BIBLE PROOFS
A Fireside Aid for Teaching Christians

Compiled by
Nabil I. Hanna

KALIMÁT PRESS
LOS ANGELES

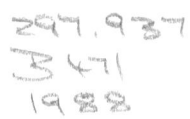

Copyright © 1988 by Kalimát Press
All Rights Reserved
Manufactured in the United States of America

Library of Congress Cataloguing in Publication Data
Bible proofs: A fireside aid for teaching Christians
compiled by Nabil I. Hanna.
p. 176   21 cm.
Includes bibliographical references (pp. 159-160)
ISBN 0-933770-66-9 : $14.95
1. Bahai Faith—Relations—Christianity. 2. Christianity and other religions—Bahai Faith. 3. Bible—Bahai interpretations.
I. Hanna, Nabil I.
BP377.B53 1990
297'.937—dc20

Acknowledgments

Selections from the Bible are taken from the Revised Standard Version of the Old and New Testaments.

Extracts from the following works are reprinted by permission of the National Spiritual Assembly of the Bahá'ís of the United States: By Bahá'u'lláh, *Epistle to the Son of the Wolf,* Copyright 1941, 1953, © 1971; *Gleanings from the Writings of Bahá'u'lláh,* Copyright 1939, 1952, © 1976; *The Kitáb-i-Iqán. The Book of Certitude,* Copyright 1931, © 1950. By 'Abdu'l-Bahá, *The Promulgation of Universal Peace,* Copyright © 1982; *Secret of Divine Civilization,* Copyright 1957, © 1970; *Some Answered Questions,* Copyright 1930, 1954, © 1964, 1981; *Tablets of Abdu'l-Baha.* From
continued on page 161

He, verily, is come with His Kingdom, and all the atoms cry aloud: "Lo! The Lord is come in His great majesty!" He who is the Father is come, and the Son (Jesus), in the holy vale, crieth out: "Here am I, here am I, O Lord, My God!" whilst Sinai circleth round the House, and the Burning Bush calleth aloud: "The All-Bounteous is come mounted upon the clouds!"

Bahá'u'lláh
The Proclamation of Bahá'u'lláh, p. 27

CONTENTS

Preface *by Nabil I. Hanna*

PART ONE: HE WHO WAS PROMISED
The Coming of the Promised One 1
The Signs of His Coming 9
He Comes in the Clouds 19
The Place He Will Appear 23
The Time of His Coming 29
He Comes as a Thief 39
He Comes with a New Name 43
The Unity of God and His Manifestations 49

PART TWO: SOME CHRISTIAN SUBJECTS
The Word of God 57
Salvation! 63
Baptism 67
The Lord's Supper 71
Resurrection and Judgment Day 77
The Meaning of "Life" and "Death" 83
The Symbolic Meanings of Parables 89
The Mission of Christ 97
The Miracles of Christ 103
The Ascension of Christ 109
Jesus, the Son of God 117
Was Jesus the Only One Who Had No Father? 123
The Meaning of Anti-Christ 129

PART THREE: THE PLAN OF GOD

Opposition to the Prophets of God 135
The Select Few 143
Two Prophets to Appear 147
The Man Whose Name Is the Branch 151
Future Manifestations of God 155

Selected Bibliography 159

PREFACE

The purpose of this book is to enable the reader to construe the meanings of some selected verses of the Bible which, for Bahá'ís, clearly establish the fact that Bahá'u'lláh is the Promised One (that is, the Father, the Spirit of Truth, the Comforter, the Messiah, the Qá'im, the Avatar, etc.) awaited by the majority of the people on earth. The collection is intended as an aid to gentle fireside teaching or for deepening classes. 'Abdu'l-Bahá has mentioned that such Bible verses as are included here should be collected and memorized:

> It is very good to memorize the logical points and the proofs of the Holy Books. Those proofs and evidences which establish the fact that Bahá'u'lláh is the fulfillment of the Promises of the Holy Book. These proofs ought to be collected and memorized.
> (quoted in *Star of the West*, Vol. 3, No. 11, Sept. 27, 1912)

The chapters of this book deal with the significant topics which most often come up during Bahá'í meetings when the discussion turns to Christian topics. The central Bahá'í claim that Bahá'u'lláh fulfils the prophecies and expectations that Christians hold concerning their Promised One inevitably gives rise to questions about "the signs of the times," "a new name," "salvation," "resurrection," and so forth.

PREFACE

The brief introduction to the selected verses at the beginning of each chapter is not intended to explain in detail the meanings of the quotations, but only to introduce the topic and leave the elaboration of the theme to the fireside speaker or discussion leader. Many of the verses really need no explanation, especially when compared to the other quotes under a given topic. Some passages serve as a guide to understand the inner meanings of other more abstruse passages.

Bahá'í quotations have been added after the Bible passages to clarify and expound upon what has already been alluded to in the Bible. These passages elucidate the unity of God, the unity of His Messages and Manifestations, and give the reader an opportunity to compare biblical and Bahá'í teachings on a given topic.

Naturally, Bahá'ís should always take care not to be drawn into futile arguments over the different interpretations of the Bible that are made by various Christian sects. Rather, they should become acquainted with the inner meanings of the Scriptures and share these with others in a spirit of understanding and loving consideration. 'Abdu'l-Bahá has explained:

> All the texts and teachings of the Holy Testaments have intrinsic spiritual meanings. They are not to be taken literally. I therefore pray in your behalf that you may be given the power of understanding these inner real meanings of the Holy Scriptures and may become informed of the mysteries deposited in the words of the Bible so that you may attain eternal life

and that your hearts may be attracted to the Kingdom of God.
> (*The Divine Art of Living,* p. 40)

And also:

> I beg of God through the confirmation and assistance of the True One thou mayest show the utmost eloquence, fluency, ability and skill in teaching the real significance of the Bible.
> (*Tablets of Abdul-Baha,* vol. 2, p. 243)

The aim of any true teaching is not disputation or argument. The intent of the teacher should not be to demonstrate to the seeker that he is wrong, but rather to guide him gradually toward the truth. Bahá'u'lláh drew the attention of the believers to the example of 'Abdu'l-Bahá as a teacher:

> A pleasing, kindly disposition and a display of tolerance towards the people are requisites of teaching the Cause. Whatever a person says, hollow and product of vain imaginings and a parrot-like repetition of somebody else's views though it be, one ought to let it pass. One should not engage in disputation leading to and ending with obstinate refusal and hostility, because the other person would consider himself worsted and defeated. Consequently further veils intervene between him and the Cause, and he becomes more negligent of it. One ought to say: right, admitted, but look at the

matter in this other way, and judge for yourself whether it is true or false; of course it should be said with courtesy, with kindliness, with consideration. Then the other person will listen, will not seek to answer back and to marshal proofs in repudiation. He will agree, because he comes to realize that the purpose has not been to engage in verbal battle and to gain mastery over him. He sees that the purpose has been to impart the word of truth, to show humanity, to bring forth heavenly qualities. His eyes and his ears are opened, his heart responds, his true nature unfolds, and by the grace of God, he becomes a new creation... The Most Great Branch ['Abdu'l-Bahá] gives a willing ear to any manner of senseless talk, to such an extent that the other person says to himself: He is trying to learn from me. Then, gradually, by such means as the other person cannot perceive, He gives him insight and understanding.
(quoted in *'Abdu'l-Bahá*, p. 27)

One will notice that the life of 'Abdu'l-Bahá, His day to day living, cannot be separated from the manner in which He taught the Faith. It is the same thing with our own lives—the more we improve our spiritual lives, the more our deeds reflect the attributes of God developed within us, the more we are enabled to memorize the passages and quotations that establish the fact that Bahá'u'lláh is the fulfillment of all the religions of the past, and the better instruments we become for the Light of God to flow through us to others.

PART ONE:

HE WHO WAS PROMISED

THE PEARL OF GREAT PRICE
"Again, the kingdom of heaven is like a merchant in search of fine pearls, who, on finding one pearl of great value, went and sold all that he had and bought it." (Matthew 13:45)

THE COMING OF THE PROMISED ONE

The Holy Bible speaks of the coming of a Promised Day and alludes to it in many passages. This is also true of the sacred books of all other religions. The various prophecies concerning this glorious time are very similar: There will come a Day when the Kingdom of God will be established and His "will be done, on earth as it is in heaven." Evil will be destroyed, the righteous will rule, and the true religion will be established. There will be no more war; it will be the end of sorrow and suffering; all the people of the world will be brought together. And all this will be accomplished by *one man*, whose miraculous advent will signal the arrival of the Promised Day. For Christians, this man is Christ returned.

In the following passages from the Bible, we notice, however, that it is not Christ Himself in the body that is coming again, but rather the Spirit of Christ—the Spirit of Truth. The Bible promises the coming of the Spirit of Truth, the Glory of the Lord, the Counselor, the Holy Spirit, the Comforter, and so forth. This is the same Spirit promised by all the religions of the past.

Biblical References

John 14:16 — "And I will pray the Father, and he will give you another Counselor, to be with you for ever, even the Spirit of truth, whom the world cannot receive, because it neither sees him or knows him . . ."

John 16:12-13 — "I have yet many things to say to you, but you cannot bear them now. When the Spirit of truth comes, he will guide you into all truth; for he will not speak on his own authority, but whatever he hears he will speak, and he will declare to you the things that are to come."

John 14:30 — "I will no longer talk much with you, for the ruler of this world is coming."

John 14:26 — "But the Counselor, the Holy Spirit, whom the Father will send in my name, he will teach you all things, and bring to your remembrance all that I have said to you."

John 15:26 — "But when the Counselor comes, whom I shall send to you from the Father, even the Spirit of truth, who proceeds from the Father, he will bear witness to me . . ."

John 16:7   "Nevertheless I tell you the truth: it is to your advantage that I go away, for if I do not go away, the Counselor will not come to you; but if I go, I will send him to you."

Bahá'í References

The Revelation which, from time immemorial, hath been acclaimed as the Purpose and Promise of all the Prophets of God, and the most cherished Desire of His Messengers, hath now, by virtue of the pervasive Will of the Almighty and at His irresistible bidding, been revealed unto men. The advent of such a Revelation hath been heralded in all the sacred Scriptures.

Bahá'u'lláh
Gleanings, p. 5

The time fore-ordained unto the peoples and kindreds of the earth is now come. The promises of God, as recorded in the holy Scriptures, have all been fulfilled. Out of Zion hath gone forth the Law of God, and Jerusalem, and the hills and the land thereof, are filled with the glory of His Revelation. Happy is the man that pondereth in his heart that which hath been revealed in the Books of God, the Help in Peril, the Self-Subsisting.

Bahá'u'lláh
Gleanings, pp. 12-13

O kings of the earth! He Who is the sovereign Lord of all is come. The Kingdom is God's, the omnipotent Protector, the Self-Subsisting. Worship none but God, and, with radiant hearts, lift up your faces unto your Lord, the Lord of all names. This is a Revelation to which whatever ye possess can never be compared, could ye but know it.

Bahá'u'lláh
Kitáb-i-Aqdas, p. 17

"Followers of the Gospel," Bahá'u'lláh addressing the whole of Christendom exclaims, *"behold the gates of heaven are flung open. He that had ascended unto it is now come. Give ear to His voice calling aloud over land and sea, announcing to all mankind the advent of this Revelation—a Revelation through the agency of which the Tongue of Grandeur is now proclaiming: 'Lo, the sacred Pledge hath been fulfilled, for He, the Promised One, is come!'" "The voice of the Son of Man is calling aloud from the sacred vale: 'Here am I, here am I, O God my God!' . . . whilst from the Burning Bush breaketh forth the cry: 'Lo, the Desire of the world is made manifest in His transcendent glory!' The Father hath come. That which ye were promised in the Kingdom of God is fulfilled. This is the Word*

which the Son veiled when He said to those around Him that at that time they could not bear it . . . Verily the Spirit of Truth is come to guide you unto all truth . . . He is the One Who glorified the Son and exalted His Cause . . ." *"The Comforter Whose advent all the scriptures have promised is now come that He may reveal unto you all knowledge and wisdom. Seek Him over the entire surface of the earth, haply ye may find him."*

Bahá'u'lláh, quoted in
The World Order of Bahá'u'lláh, pp. 104-105

To Him Jesus Christ had referred as the *"Prince of this World,"* as the *"Comforter"* Who will *"reprove the world of sin, and of righteousness, and of judgment,"* as the *"Spirit of Truth"* Who *"shall not speak of Himself, but whatsoever He shall hear, that shall He speak,"* as the *"Lord of the Vineyard,"* and as the *"Son of Man"* Who *"shall come in the glory of His Father"* *"in the clouds of heaven with power and great glory,"* with *"all the holy angels"* about Him, and *"all nations"* gathered before His throne. To Him the Author of the Apocalypse had alluded as the *"Glory of the God,"* as *"Alpha and Omega,"* *"the Beginning and the End,"* *"the First and the Last."* Identifying His Revelation with the *"third woe,"* he, moreover, had extolled His Law as *"a new heaven and a new earth,"* as the *"Tabernacle of God,"* as the *"Holy City,"* as the *"New Jerusalem, coming down from God out of heaven, prepared as a bride adorned for her husband."* To His Day Jesus Christ Himself had referred as *"the regeneration when the Son of Man shall sit in the throne of His glory."* To the hour of His advent St. Paul had alluded as the hour of the "last trump," the "trump of God," whilst St. Peter had spoken of it as the "Day of God, wherein the heavens being on fire shall be dissolved, and the elements shall melt with fervent heat." His Day, he, furthermore, had described as "the times of refreshing," "the times of restitution of all things, which God hath spoken by the mouth of all His holy Prophets since the world began."

Shoghi Effendi
God Passes By, pp. 95-96

To Him Isaiah, the greatest of the Jewish prophets, had alluded as the *"Glory of the Lord,"* the *"Everlasting Father,"* the *"Prince of Peace,"* the *"Wonderful,"* the *"Counsellor,"* the *"Rod come forth out of the stem of Jesse"* and the *"Branch grown out of His roots,"* Who *"shall be established upon the throne of David,"* Who *"will come with strong hand,"* Who *"shall judge among the nations,"* Who *"shall smite the earth with the rod of His mouth, and with the breath of His lips slay the wicked,"* and Who *"shall assemble the outcasts of Israel, and gather together the dispersed of Judah from the four corners of the earth."* Of Him David had sung in his Psalms, acclaiming Him as the *"Lord of Hosts"* and the *"King of Glory."* To Him Haggai had referred as the *"Desire of all nations,"* and Zachariah as the *"Branch"* Who *"shall grow up out of His place,"* and *"shall build the Temple of the Lord."* Ezekiel had extolled Him as the *"Lord"* Who *"shall be king over all the earth,"* while to His day Joel and Zephaniah had both referred as the *"day of Jehovah,"* the latter describing it as *"a day of wrath, a day of trouble and distress, a day of wasteness and desolation, a day of darkness and gloominess, a day of clouds and thick darkness, a day of the trumpet and alarm against the fenced cities, and against the high towers."* His Day Ezekiel and Daniel had, moreover, both acclaimed as the *"day of the Lord,"* and Malachi described as *"the great and dreadful day of the Lord"* when *"the Sun of Righteousness"* will *"arise, with healing in His wings,"* whilst Daniel had pronounced His advent as signalizing the end of the *"abomination that maketh desolate."*

Shoghi Effendi
God Passes By, pp. 94-95

O thou who art waiting, tarry no longer, for He is come. Behold His Tabernacle and His Glory dwelling therein. It is the Ancient Glory, with a new Manifestation.

Bahá'u'lláh, quoted in
Bahá'u'lláh and the New Era, p. 23

THE LAST JUDGMENT
(An Artist's Conception)

THE SIGNS OF HIS COMING

The Holy Scriptures have given us many signs to watch for which will signal the advent of the Promised Day. Among these signs are: changes in the heavens, the restoration of the fortunes of Israel, the Gospel preached throughout the world, the spread of decadence and immorality, the decline of religion, and so on. Anyone who studies this question will notice that the signs mentioned have all become a reality.

Although the existence of some of these signs is obvious, others must be regarded from a spiritual perspective. How could the sun be literally darkened, or the moon cease to shine? Even if this were to happen, there would be no light to see the promised Return, and we would all die without the heat of the sun. Stars falling from heaven? This could probably be done in a Hollywood production studio, if we plan to live in a world of fantasy. But every star is many millions of times larger than our planet. No star could even approach the earth without the world being destroyed.

The Bahá'í Writings teach us that these signs each have inner spiritual meanings that must be unravelled.

Biblical References

Isaiah
13:9-16

Behold, the day of the LORD comes,
   cruel, with wrath and fierce anger,
to make the earth a desolation
   and to destroy its sinners from it.
For the stars of the heavens and their
     constellations,
   will not give their light;
the sun will be dark at its rising
   and the moon will not shed its
     light.
I will punish the world for its evil,
   and the wicked for their iniquity;
I will put an end to the pride of the
     arrogant,
   and lay low the haughtiness of the
     ruthless.
I will make men more rare than fine
     gold,
   and mankind than the gold of
     Ophir.
Therefore, I will make the heavens
     tremble,
   and the earth will be shaken out of
     its place,
at the wrath of the LORD of hosts
   in the day of his fierce anger.

Amos
9:14-15

"I will restore the fortunes of my
   people Israel,

and they shall rebuild the ruined
  cities and inhabit them;
they shall plant vineyards and drink
  their wine,
  and they shall make gardens and
    eat their fruit.
I will plant them upon their land,
  and they shall never again be
    plucked up
  out of the land which I have
    given them,"
            says the LORD your God.

Daniel 12:1 "At that time shall arise Michael, the great prince who has charge of your people, and there shall be a time of trouble, such as never has been since there was a nation till that time; but at that time your people shall be delivered, every one whose name shall be found written in the book."

Mark 13:7-10 "And when you hear of wars and rumors of wars, do not be alarmed; this must take place, but the end is not yet. For nation will rise against nation, and kingdom against kingdom; there will be earthquakes in various places, there will be famines; this is but the beginning of the birth-pangs.

"But take heed to yourselves; for they will deliver you up to councils; and you will be beaten in synagogues; and you will stand before governors and kings for my sake, to bear testimony before them. And the gospel must first be preached to all nations."

Matthew 24:29-31 "Immediately after the tribulation of those days the sun will be darkened, and the moon will not give its light, and the stars will fall from heaven, and the powers of the heavens will be shaken; then will appear the sign of the Son of man in heaven, and then all the tribes of the earth will mourn, and they will see the Son of man coming on the clouds of heaven with power and great glory; and he will send out his angels with a loud trumpet call, and they will gather his elect from the four winds, from one end of heaven to the other."

Luke 21:25 "And there will be signs in sun and moon and stars, and upon the earth distress of nations in perplexity at the roaring of the sea and the waves, men fainting with fear and with foreboding of what is coming on the world;

for the powers of the heavens will be shaken."

Matthew 24:14 — "And this gospel of the kingdom will be preached throughout the whole world, as a testimony to all nations; and then the end will come."

Matthew 24:21-22 — "For then there will be great tribulation, such as has not been from the beginning of the world until now, no, and never will be. And if those days had not been shortened, no human being would be saved; but for the sake of the elect those days will be shortened."

2 Timothy 3:1-5 — But understand this, that in the last days there will come times of stress. For men will be lovers of self, lovers of money, proud, arrogant, abusive, disobedient to their parents, ungrateful, unholy, inhuman, implacable slanderers, profligates, fierce, haters of good, treacherous, reckless, swollen with conceit, lovers of pleasure rather than lovers of God, holding the form of religion but denying the power of it. Avoid such people.

Bahá'í References

And now, concerning His words— "The sun shall be darkened, and the moon shall not give light, and the stars shall fall from heaven." By the terms "sun" and "moon," mentioned in the writings of the Prophets of God, is not meant solely the sun and moon of the visible universe. Nay rather, manifold are the meanings they have intended for these terms. In every instance they have attached to them a particular significance. Thus, by the "sun" in one sense is meant those Suns of Truth Who rise from the dayspring of ancient glory, and fill the world with a liberal effusion of grace from on high. These Suns of Truth are the universal Manifestations of God . . . Thus it is that through the rise of these Luminaries of God the world is made new, the waters of everlasting life stream forth, the billows of loving-kindness surge, the clouds of grace are gathered, and the breeze of bounty bloweth upon all created things. It is the warmth that these Luminaries of God generate, and the undying fires they kindle, which cause the light of the love of God to burn fiercely in the heart of humanity. It is through the abundant grace of these Symbols of Detachment that the Spirit of life everlasting is breathed into the bodies of the dead. Assuredly the visible sun is but a sign of the splendour of that Day-star of Truth, that Sun Which can never have a peer, a likeness, or rival.

Bahá'u'lláh
Kitáb-i-Iqán, pp. 33-34

That the term "sun" hath been applied to the leaders of religion is due to their lofty position, their fame, and renown. Such are the universally recognized divines of every age, who speak with authority, and whose fame is securely established. If they be in the likeness of the Sun of Truth, they will surely be accounted as the most exalted of all luminaries; otherwise, they are to be recognized as the focal centres of hellish fire.

... by the words "the sun shall be darkened, and the moon shall not give her light, and the stars shall fall from heaven" is intended the waywardness of the divines, and the annulment of laws firmly established by divine Revelation, all of which, in symbolic language, have been foreshadowed by the Manifestation of God. None except the righteous shall partake of this cup, none but the godly can share therein.

Bahá'u'lláh
Kitáb-i-Iqán, pp. 37 and 41

In like manner, strive thou to comprehend from these lucid, these powerful, conclusive, and unequivocal statements the meaning of the "cleaving of the heaven"—one of the signs that must needs herald the coming of the last Hour, the Day of Resurrection. As He hath said: "When the heaven shall be cloven asunder." By "heaven" is meant the heaven of divine Revelation, which is elevated with every Manifestation, and rent asunder with every subsequent one. By "cloven asunder" is meant that the former Dispensation is superseded and annulled. I swear by God! That this heaven being cloven asunder is, to the discerning, an act mightier than the cleaving of the skies!

Bahá'u'lláh
Kitáb-i-Iqán, p. 44

And now, with reference to His words: "And then shall all the tribes of the earth mourn, and they shall see the Son of man coming in the clouds of heaven with power and great glory." These words signify that in those days men will lament the loss of the Sun of the divine beauty, of the Moon of knowledge, and of the Stars of divine wisdom. Thereupon, they will behold the countenance of the promised One, the adored Beauty, descending from heaven and riding upon the clouds. By this is meant that the divine Beauty will be made manifest from the heaven of the will of God, and will appear in the form of the human temple. The term "heaven" denoteth loftiness and exaltation, inasmuch as it is the seat of the revelation of those Manifestations of Holiness, the Day-springs of ancient glory. These ancient Beings, though delivered from the womb of their mother, have in reality descended from the heaven of the will of God. Though they be dwelling on this earth, yet their true habitations are the retreats of glory in the realms above. Whilst walking amongst mortals, they soar in the heaven of the divine presence.

Bahá'u'lláh
Kitáb-i-Iqán, pp. 66-67

The Book of Isaiah announces that the Messiah will conquer the East and the West, and all nations of the world will come under His shadow, that His Kingdom will be established, that He will come from an unknown place, that the sinners will be judged, and that justice will prevail to such a degree that the wolf and the lamb, the leopard and the kid, the sucking child and the asp, shall all gather at one spring, and in one meadow, and one dwelling. The first coming was also under these conditions, though outwardly none of them came to pass. Therefore, the Jews rejected Christ . . .

The second coming of Christ also will be in like manner: the signs and conditions which have been spoken of all have meanings, and are not to be taken literally. Among other things it is said that the stars will fall upon the earth. The stars are endless and innumerable, and modern mathematicians have established and proved scientifically that the globe of the sun is estimated to be about one million and a half times greater than the earth, and each of the stars to be a thousand times larger than the sun. If these stars were to fall upon the surface of the earth, how could they find place there? It would be as though a thousand million of Himalaya mountains were to fall upon a grain of mustard seed. According to reason and science this thing is quite impossible. What is even more strange is that Christ said: "Perhaps I shall come when you are yet asleep, for the coming of the Son of man is like the coming of a thief." Perhaps the thief will be in the house, and the owner will not know it.

'Abdu'l-Bahá
Some Answered Questions, pp. 111-12

HE COMES IN THE CLOUDS

The Bible tells us that the promised Redeemer will come to earth "in the clouds," "on the clouds," or "with the clouds." Even if we take this prophecy literally, it would be clear that if anyone descended from heaven in clouds—he would be hidden *by those clouds* from sight. A savior riding on a cloud could not be seen by those below on earth.

The Bahá'í Writings explain the meaning of the "clouds" mentioned in the Bible. They are the barriers which prevent humanity from recognizing the true Prophets of God. They are clouds of prejudice and pride and idle fancy, clouds of tradition and man-made dogma—anything which stands between the believer and the true messenger of God.

Biblical References

Mark 13:25-26	". . . and the stars will be falling from heaven, and the powers in the heavens will be shaken. And then they will see the Son of man coming in clouds with great power and glory."

Mark 14:61-62	Again the high priest asked him, "Are you the Christ, the Son of the Blessed?" And Jesus said, "I am; and you will see the Son of man seated at the right hand of Power, and coming with the clouds of heaven."
Matthew 24:30	". . . then will appear the sign of the Son of man in heaven, and then all the tribes of the earth will mourn, and they will see the Son of man coming on the clouds of heaven with power and great glory."
Luke 21:27	"And then they will see the Son of man coming in a cloud with power and great glory."
Revelation 1:7	Behold, he is coming with the clouds . . .

Bahá'í References

It is evident that the changes brought about in every Dispensation constitute the dark clouds that intervene between the eye of man's understanding and the divine Luminary which shineth forth from the dayspring of the divine Essence. Consider how men for generations have been blindly imitating their fathers, and have been trained according to such ways and manners as have been laid down by the dictates of their Faith. Were these men, therefore, to discover suddenly that a Man, Who hath been living in their midst, Who, with respect to every human limitation, hath been their equal, had risen to abolish every established principle imposed by their Faith—principles by which for centuries they have been disciplined, and every opposer and denier of which they have come to regard as infidel, profligate and wicked,—they would of a certainty be veiled and hindered from acknowledging His truth. Such things are as "clouds" that veil the eyes of those whose inner being hath not tasted the Salsabíl of detachment, nor drunk from the Kawthar of the knowledge of God.

Bahá'u'lláh
Kitáb-i-Iqán, pp. 73-74

By the term "clouds" is meant those things that are contrary to the ways and desires of men. . . . These "clouds" signify, in one sense, the annulment of laws, the abrogation of former Dispensations, the repeal of rituals and customs current amongst men, the exalting of the illiterate faithful above the learned opposers of the Faith. In another sense, they mean the appearance of that immortal Beauty in the image of mortal man, with such human limitations as eating and drinking, poverty and riches, glory and abasement, sleeping and waking, and such other things as cast doubt in the minds of men, and cause them to turn away. All such veils are symbolically referred to as "clouds." These are the "clouds" that cause the heavens of the knowledge and understanding of all that dwell on earth to be cloven asunder. Even as He hath revealed: "On that day shall the heaven be cloven by the clouds." Even as the clouds prevent the eyes of man from beholding the sun, so do these things hinder the souls of men from recognizing the light of the divine Luminary.

Bahá'u'lláh
Kitáb-i-Iqán, pp. 71-72

And they are waiting for Him to come down from there again, riding upon a cloud, and they imagine that there are clouds in that infinite space and that He will ride thereon and by that means He will decend. Whereas the truth is that a cloud is but a vapour that riseth out of the earth, and it doth not come down from heaven. Rather, the cloud referred to in the Gospel is the human body, so called because the body is as a veil to man, which, even as a cloud, preventeth him from beholding the Sun of Truth that shineth from the horizon of Christ.

'Abdu'l-Bahá
*Selections from the
Writings of 'Abdu'l-Bahá,* p. 168

THE PLACE HE WILL APPEAR

The prophecies in the Holy Scriptures conspicuously indicate the place where the Promised One is to appear. Reading the history of the Bahá'í Faith, and meditating on the following passages, it is clear that the banishments of Bahá'u'lláh fulfill these prophecies. From Tehran, the capital of Iran, "east" of the Holy Land, Bahá'u'lláh was banished to Baghdad. From there He was sent to Constantinople (Istanbul) and then to Adrianople (Edirne) and finally—by way of Egypt—to the prison city of 'Akká.

Bahá'u'lláh's name translates as the "Glory of God" or the "Glory of the Lord." The importance that Isaiah gives to Mount Carmel and the plain of Sharon (south of Mt. Carmel)—which he promises will see the "Glory of the Lord"—provides another indication of the location of the appearance of the Promised One.

Biblical References

Ezekiel 43:1-2	Afterward he brought me to the gate, the gate facing east. And behold, the

glory of the God of Israel came from the east . . .

Amos 1:2
"The LORD roars from Zion,
    and utters his voice from Jerusalem;
the pastures of the shepherds mourn,
    and the top of Carmel withers."

Ezekiel 43: 4-5
As the glory of the LORD entered the temple by the gate facing east, the Spirit lifted me up, and brought me into the inner court; and behold, the glory of the LORD filled the temple.

Ezekiel 3:22-23
And the hand of the LORD was there upon me; and he said to me, "Arise, go forth into the plain, and there I will speak with you." So I arose and went forth into the plain; and, lo, the glory of the LORD stood there, like the glory which I had seen by the river Chebar; and I fell on my face.

Micah 7:11-13
A day for the building of your walls!
    In that day the boundary shall be far extended.
In that day they will come to you,
    from Assyria to Egypt,
and from Egypt to the River,

        from sea to sea and from
          mountain to mountain.
But the earth will be desolate
    because of its inhabitants,
    for the fruit of their doings.

Isaiah 35:1-2   The wilderness and the dry land
        shall be glad,
    the desert shall rejoice and blossom;
        like the crocus it shall blossom
          abundantly,
        and rejoice with joy and singing.
    The glory of Lebanon shall be given
        to it,
        the majesty of Carmel and Sharon.
    They shall see the glory of the Lord,
        the majesty of our God.

Isaiah 2:2-4   It shall come to pass in the latter days
        that the mountain of the house of
          the Lord
    shall be established as the highest of
        the mountains,
    and shall be raised above the hills;
    and all the nations shall flow to it,
        and many peoples shall come, and
          say:
    "Come, let us go up to the mountain
        of the Lord,
        to the house of the God of Jacob;

> that he may teach us his ways
> and that we may walk in his paths."
> For out of Zion shall go forth the law,
> and the word of the LORD from Jerusalem.
> He shall judge between the nations,
> and shall decide for many peoples;
> and they shall beat their swords into plowshares,
> and their spears into pruning hooks;
> nation shall not lift up sword against nation,
> neither shall they learn war any more.

Bahá'í References

Call out to Zion, O Carmel, and announce the joyful tidings: He that was hidden from mortal eyes is come!

Bahá'u'lláh
Gleanings, p. 16

The Sun of Truth shineth resplendently, at the bidding of the Lord of the kingdom of utterance, and the King of the heaven of knowledge, above the horizon of the prison-city of 'Akká. Repudiation hath not veiled it, and ten thousand hosts arrayed against it were powerless to withhold it from shining. Thou canst excuse thyself no longer. Either thou must recognize it, or—God forbid—arise and deny all the Prophets!

Bahá'u'lláh
Epistle to the Son of the Wolf, p. 119

Hearken with thine inner ear unto the Voice of Jeremiah, Who saith: "Oh, for great is that Day, and it hath no equal." Wert thou to observe with the eye of fairness, thou wouldst perceive the greatness of the Day. Incline thine ear unto the Voice of this All-Knowing Counsellor, and suffer not thyself to be deprived of the mercy that hath surpassed all created things, visible and invisible. Lend an ear unto the song of David. He saith: "Who will bring me into the Strong City?" The Strong City is 'Akká which hath been named the Most Great Prison, and which possesseth a fortress and mighty ramparts.

Bahá'u'lláh
Epistle to the Son of the Wolf, p. 144

Carmel, in the Book of God, hath been designated as the Hill of God, and His Vineyard. It is here that, by the grace of the Lord of Revelation, the Tabernacle of Glory hath been raised. Happy are they that attain thereunto; happy they that set their faces towards it.

Bahá'u'lláh
Epistle to the Son of the Wolf, p. 145

... Bahá'u'lláh's tent, the *"Tabernacle of Glory,"* was raised on Mt. Carmel, *"the Hill of God and His Vineyard,"* the home of Elijah, extolled by Isaiah as the *"mountain of the Lord,"* to which *"all nations shall flow."*

Shoghi Effendi
God Passes By, p. 194

"'Akká, itself, flanked by the *"glory of Lebanon,"* and lying in full view of the *"splendor of Carmel,"* at the foot of the hills which enclose the home of Jesus Christ Himself, had been described by David as *"the Strong City,"* designated by Hosea as *"a door of hope,"* and alluded to by Ezekiel as *"the gate that looketh towards the East,"* whereunto *"the glory of the God of Israel came from the way of the East,"* His voice *"like a noise of many waters."*

Shoghi Effendi
God Passes By, p. 184

THE TIME OF HIS COMING

Although the Bible contains many references to the time of the coming of the Promised One, for the sake of simplicity and quick reference, this chapter will concern itself with only one of them. This one is the well-known prophecy found in the Book of Daniel that was confirmed by Jesus in the Gospel of Matthew.

Daniel says that from the time of the decree to rebuild Jerusalem (457 B.C.) to the end of the abomination of desolation, there were to be 2,300 days. According to the Bible, each day counts as a year. (Numbers 14:34; Ezekiel 4:6) After seven weeks and sixty-two weeks (483 days), the Messiah (the annointed one) would be cut off. At the end of the 2,300 days, the sanctuary would be restored.

From the issuing of the decree in 457 B.C. until the birth of Christ, there were 456 years. Subtracting 456 from 483 leaves the year 27 A.D. as the date of the crucifixion of Christ. Subtracting 456 from 2,300, leaves 1844 A.D. as the end of the abomination of desolation.

The year 1844 A.D. is equivalent to the Islamic calendar year of 1260 A.H., the year the Bahá'í Faith began.

BIBLE PROOFS

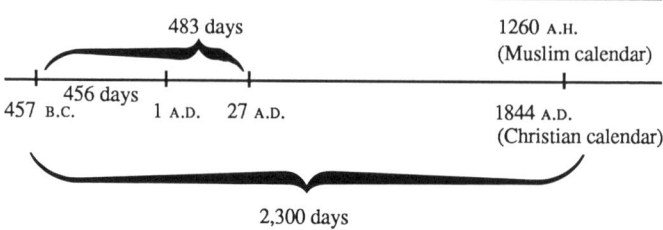

Biblical References

Daniel 8:13-14 — Then I heard a holy one speaking; and another holy one said to the one that spoke, "For how long is the vision concerning the continual burnt offering, the transgression that makes desolate, and the giving over of the sanctuary and host to be trampled under foot?" And he said to him, "For two thousand and three hundred evenings and mornings; then the sanctuary shall be restored to its rightful state."

Daniel 9:25-26 — "Know therefore and understand that from the going forth of the word to restore and build Jerusalem to the coming of an anointed one, a prince, there shall be seven weeks. Then for sixty-two weeks it shall be built again with squares and moat . . . And after the sixty-two weeks, an anointed one shall be cut off . . ."

THE TIME

Matthew 24:2-3, 15

"Truly, I say to you, there will not be left here one stone upon another, that will not be thrown down."

As he sat on the Mount of Olives, the disciples came to him privately, saying, "Tell us, when will this be, and what will be the sign of your coming and of the close of the age?" . . .

"So when you see the desolating sacrilege spoken of by the prophet Daniel, standing in the holy place (let the reader understand) . . ."

Daniel 12:6-7

And I said to the man clothed in linen, who was above the waters of the stream, "How long shall it be till the end of these wonders?" The man clothed in linen, who was above the waters of the stream, raised his right hand and his left hand toward heaven; and I heard him swear by him who lives for ever that it would be for a time, two times, and half a time . . .

Daniel 12:11-12

And from the time that the continual burnt offering is taken away, and the abomination that makes desolate is set up, there shall be a thousand two hundred and ninety days. Blessed is he who waits and comes to the

	thousand three hundred and thirty-five days.
Revelation 12:5-6	... she brought forth a male child, one who is to rule all the nations with a rod of iron, but her child was caught up to God and to his throne, and the woman fled into the wilderness, where she has a place prepared by God, in which to be nourished for one thousand two hundred and sixty days.

Bahá'í References

But Daniel mentions two dates. One of these dates begins with the command of Artaxerxes to Ezra to rebuild Jerusalem; this is the seventy weeks which came to an end with the ascension of Christ, when by His martyrdom the sacrifice and oblation ceased.

The second period, which is found in the twenty-sixth verse, means that after the termination of the rebuilding of Jerusalem until the ascension of Christ, there will be sixty-two weeks, seven weeks are the duration of the rebuilding of Jerusalem, which took forty-nine years. When you add these seven weeks to the sixty-two weeks, it makes sixty-nine weeks, and in the last week (69-70) the ascension of Christ took place. These seventy weeks are thus completed, and there is no contradiction.

Now that the manifestation of Christ has been proved by the prophecies of Daniel, let us prove the manifestation of Bahá'u'lláh and the Báb. Up to the present we have only mentioned rational proofs; now we shall speak of traditional proofs.

In the eighth chapter of the Book of Daniel, verse thirteen, it is said: "Then I heard one saint speaking, and another saint said unto that certain saint which spake, How long shall be the vision concerning the daily sacrifice, and the transgression of desolation, to give both the sanctuary and the host to be trodden under foot?" Then he answered (v. 14): "Unto two thousand and three hundred days; then shall the sanctuary be cleansed"; (v. 17) "But he said unto me . . . at the time of the end shall be the vision." That is to say, how long will this misfortune, this ruin, this abasement and degradation last? meaning, when will be the dawn of the Manifestation? Then he answered, "Two thousand and three hundred days; then shall the sanctuary be cleansed." Briefly, the purport of this passage is that he appoints two thousand three hundred years, for in the text of the Bible each day is a year. Then from the date of the issuing of the decree of Artaxerxes to rebuild Jerusalem until the day of the birth of Christ there are 456 years, and from the birth of Christ until the day of the manifestation of the Báb there are 1844 years. When you add 456 years to this number it makes 2300 years. That is to say, the fulfillment of the vision of Daniel took place in the year A.D. 1844, and this is the year of the Báb's manifestation according to the actual text of the Book of Daniel. Consider how clearly he determines the year of the manifestation; there could be no clearer prophecy for a manifestation than this.

In Matthew, chapter 24 verse 3, Christ clearly says that what Daniel meant by this prophecy was the date of the manifestation, and this is the verse: "And he sat upon the Mount of Olives, the disciples came unto him privately, saying, Tell us, when shall these things be? and what shall be the sign of thy coming, and of the end of the world?" One of the explanations he gave them in reply was this (v. 15): "When ye therefore shall see the abomination of desolation, spoken of by Daniel the prophet, stand in the holy place, (whoso readeth let him understand)." In this answer he referred them to the eighth chapter of the Book of Daniel, saying that every one who reads it will understand that it is this time that is spoken of. Consider how clearly the manifestation of the Báb is spoken of in the Old Testament and in the Gospel.

To conclude, let us now explain the date of the manifestation of Bahá'u'lláh from the Bible. The date of Báha'u'lláh is calculated according to lunar years from the mission of and the Hejira of Muhammad; for in the religion of Muhammad the lunar year is in use, as also it is the lunar year which is employed concerning all commands of worship.

In Daniel, chapter 12, verse 6, it is said: "And one said to the man clothed in linen, which was upon the waters of the river, How long shall it be to the end of these wonders? And I heard the man clothed in linen, which was upon the waters of the river, when he held up his right hand and his left hand unto heaven, and sware by him that liveth for ever that it shall be for a time, times, and a half; and that when he shall have accomplished to scatter the power of the holy people, all these things shall be finished."

As I have already explained the signification of one day, it is not necessary to explain it further; but we will say briefly that each day of the Father counts as a year, and in each year there are twelve months. Thus three years and a half make forty-two months, and forty-two months are twelve hundred and sixty days. The Báb, the precursor to Bahá'u'lláh, appeared in the year 1260 from the Hejira of Muhammad, by the reckoning of Islam.

Afterwards, in verse 11, it is said: "And from the time that the daily sacrifice shall be taken away, and the abomination that maketh desolation be set up, there shall be a thousand two hundred and ninety days. Blessed is he that waiteth and cometh to the thousand three hundred and five-and-thirty days."

The beginning of this lunar reckoning is from the day of the proclamation of the prophethood of Muhammad in the country of Hijáz; and that was three years after his mission, because in the beginning the prophethood of Muhammad was kept secret, and no one knew it save Khadíjah and Ibn Nawfal. After three years it was announced. And Bahá'u'lláh in the year 1290 from the proclamation of the mission of Muhammad, caused His manifestation to be known.

'Abdu'l-Bahá
Some Answered Questions, pp. 41-44

Consider how the prophecies correspond to one another. In the Apocalypse, the appearance of the Promised One is appointed after forty-two months, and Daniel expresses it as three times and a half, which is also forty-two months, which are twelve hundred and sixty days. In another passage of John's Revelation it is clearly spoken of as twelve hundred and sixty days, and in the Holy Book it is said that each day signifies one year. Nothing could be more clear than this agreement of the prophecies with one another. The Báb appeared in the year 1260 of the Hejira of Muhammad, which is the beginning of the universal era-reckoning of all Islam. There are no clearer proofs than this in the Holy Books for any Manifestation. For him who is just, the agreement of the times indicated by the tongues of the Great Ones is the most conclusive proof. There is no other possible explanation of these prophecies. Blessed are the just souls who seek the truth.

'Abdu'l-Bahá
Some Answered Questions, pp. 71-72

THE WISE AND FOOLISH MAIDENS
"Watch there, for you know neither the day nor the hour."
(Matthew 25:13)

HE COMES AS A THIEF

The Scriptures, in addition to foretelling the time of His coming, have also indicated the manner in which the Promised One will come. Many passages in the Bible insist that He will come as a "thief in the night," while the people are asleep. That is, He will come secretly and unexpectedly, and the people will be unaware.

The Parable of the Ten Maidens, found in Matthew, Chapter 25, clearly demonstrates the manner of His coming. Only the faithful maidens, who had prepared for the coming of the bridegroom, were able to meet their lord with honor when he appeared unexpectedly and woke them all from their sleep. Naturally, such symbolic descriptions are not be understood literally. All of the various parables which describe the coming of the Kingdom of God cannot be acted out word for word. The parables are intended as symbolic explanations of the manner of His coming.

As at the time of Christ, the Promised Messiah was in the world, and yet the vast majority of people remained unaware.

Biblical References

Luke 17:20-21
Being asked by the Pharisees when the kingdom of God was coming, he answered them, "The kingdom of God is not coming with signs to be observed; nor will they say, 'Lo, here it is!' or 'There!' for behold, the kingdom of God is in the midst of you."

Matthew 24:42-44
"Watch therefore, for you do not know on what day your Lord is coming. But know this, that if the householder had known in what part of the night the thief was coming, he would have watched and would not have let his house be broken into. Therefore you also must be ready; for the Son of man is coming at an hour you do not expect."

Mark 13:33-37
"Take heed, watch; for you do not know when the time will come. It is like a man going on a journey, when he leaves home and puts his servants in charge, each with his work, and commands the doorkeeper to be on the watch. Watch therefore—for you do not know when the master of the house will come, in the evening, or at midnight, or at cockcrow, or in the

	morning—lest he come suddenly and find you asleep. And what I say to you I say to all: Watch!"
Revelation 3:3	"If you will not awake, I will come like a thief, and you will not know at what hour I will come upon you.'"
Revelation 16:15	("Lo, I am coming like a thief! Blessed is he who is awake, keeping his garments that he may not go naked and be seen exposed!")
2nd Peter 3:10	But the day of the Lord will come like a thief . . .
1st Thessalonians 5:2-3	For you yourselves know well that the day of the Lord will come like a thief in the night. When people say, "There is peace and security," then sudden destruction will come upon them as travail comes upon a woman with child, and there will be no escape.

Bahá'í References

. . . and still the people, even as the Messiah saith, slept on: for the day of the Manifestation, when the Lord of Hosts descended, found them wrapped in the slumber of unknowing. As He saith in the Gospel, My coming is even as when the thief is in the house, and the goodman of the house watcheth not.

'Abdu'l-Bahá
*Selections from the
Writings of 'Abdu'l-Bahá*, p. 35

All the people of the world are buried in the graves of nature, or are slumbering, heedless and unaware. Just as Christ saith: "I may come when you are not aware. The coming of the Son of Man is like the coming of a thief into a house, the owner of which is utterly unaware."

'Abdu'l-Bahá
*Selections from the
Writings of 'Abdu'l-Bahá,* pp. 198-99

... Christ said: "Perhaps I shall come when you are yet asleep, for the coming of the Son of man is like the coming of a thief." Perhaps the thief will be in the house, and the owner will not know it.

'Abdu'l-Bahá
Some Answered Questions, p. 112

HE COMES WITH A NEW NAME

In the Bible, we find the promise that, at the time of the end, the One who is expected will come bearing a new name. This often comes as a surprise to Christians, many of whom expect Christ to return to earth in the same body, with the same name, and even speaking the same words as He did the first time. But the scriptures clearly indicate that there will be a new name, and they also tell us what that name will be.

Many passages refer to the coming of "the glory of God" or "the glory of the Lord." In Arabic, these words translate as Bahá'u'lláh—the title that the Founder of the Bahá'í Faith assumed. This is the new name of the Promised One.

Biblical References

Isaiah 62:2   The nations shall see your
                  vindication,
              and all the kings your glory;
              and you shall be called by a new
                  name

which the mouth of the LORD will give.

Ezekiel 43:2-5
And behold, the glory of the God of Israel came from the east; and the sound of his coming was like the sound of many waters; and the earth shone with his glory. And the vision I saw was like the vision which I had seen when he came to destroy the city, and like the vision which I had seen by the river Chebar; and I fell upon my face. As the glory of the LORD entered the temple by the gate facing east, the Spirit lifted me up, and brought me into the inner court; and behold, the glory of the LORD filled the temple.

Isaiah 40:5
"And the glory of the LORD shall be revealed, and all flesh shall see it together, for the mouth of the LORD has spoken."

Matthew 24:4-5
And Jesus answered them, "Take heed that no one leads you astray. For many will come in my name, saying, 'I am the Christ,' and they will lead many astray."

A NEW NAME

Matthew 24:23 — "Then if any one says to you, 'Lo, here is the Christ!' or 'There he is!' do not believe it."

Revelation 2:17 — He who has an ear, let him hear what the Spirit says to the churches. To him who conquers I will give some of the hidden manna, and I will give him a white stone, with a new name written on the stone which no one knows except him who receives it.

Revelation 3:11-12 — I am coming soon; hold fast what you have, so that no one may seize your crown. He who conquers, I will make him a pillar in the temple of God; never shall he go out of it, and I will write on him the name of my God, and the name of the city of my God, the new Jerusalem which comes down from my God out of heaven, and my own new name.

Revelation 21:22-24 — And I saw no temple in the city, for its temple is the Lord God the Almighty and the Lamb. And the city has no need of sun or moon to shine upon it, for the glory of God is its light, and its lamp is the Lamb. By its light shall the nations walk; and the kings of the earth shall bring their glory into it . . .

Bahá'í References

He was formally designated Bahá'u'lláh, an appellation specifically recorded in the Persian Bayán, signifying at once the glory, the light and the splendor of God, and was styled the "Lord of Lords," the "Most Great Name," the "Ancient Beauty," the "Pen of the Most High," the "Hidden Name," the "Preserved Treasure," "He Whom God will make manifest," the "Most Great Light," the "All-Highest Horizon," the "Most Great Ocean," the "Supreme Heaven," the "Pre-Existent Root," the "Self-Subsistent," the "Day-Star of the Universe," the "Great Announcement," the "Speaker on Sinai," the "Sifter of Men," the "Wronged One of the World," the "Desire of the Nations," the "Lord of the Covenant," the "Tree beyond which there is no passing."

Shoghi Effendi
God Passes By, p. 94

To Him Isaiah, the greatest of the Jewish prophets, had alluded as the *"Glory of the Lord,"* the *"Everlasting Father,"* the *"Prince of Peace,"* the *"Wonderful,"* the *"Counsellor,"* the *"Rod come forth out of the stem of Jesse"* and the *"Branch grown out of His roots,"* Who *"shall be established upon the throne of David,"* Who *"will come with strong hand,"* Who *"shall judge among the nations,"* Who *"shall smite the earth with the rod of His mouth, and with the breath of His lips slay the wicked,"* and Who *"shall assemble the outcasts of Israel, and gather together the dispersed of Judah from the four corners of the earth."* Of Him David had sung in his Psalms, acclaiming Him as the *"Lord of Hosts"* and the *"King of Glory."*

Shoghi Effendi
God Passes By, p. 94-5

THE UNITY OF GOD AND HIS MANIFESTATIONS

All of the Messengers of God have claimed to be one and the same. They all came from the one God, with the same spirit, bringing the same spiritual teachings to different places and different peoples, at various times in history. Each prophet brought a message perfectly tailored to the time, the place, the culture to which he appeared. But, all have praised each other, all have glorified each other, all have prophesied about one another. Each prophet has explained in a different way that the messengers that come from God are, in reality, one and the same—the First and the Last, the Beginning and the End, the Return of the last one.

Each of these Divine Beings came to fulfill a specific mission for a certain age and to a particular people. To obey them in each age is to obey God; to turn away from them is to turn away from God.

Biblical References

Deuteronomy 18:17-19 — "And the L{\sc ord} said to me . . . 'I will raise up for them a prophet like you from among their brethren; and I will put my words in his mouth, and he shall speak to them all that I command him. And whoever will not give heed to my words which he shall speak in my name, I myself will require it of him.'"

Deuteronomy 33:2 — "The Lord came from Sinai,
    and dawned from Seir upon us;
  he shone forth from Mount Paran,
he came from the ten thousands of
    holy ones,
  with flaming fire at his right hand."

John 10:16 — "And I have other sheep, that are not of this fold; I must bring them also, and they will heed my voice. So there shall be one flock, one shepherd."

John 5:46 — "If you believed Moses, you would believe me, for he wrote of me. But if you do not believe his writings, how will you believe my words?"

John 10:27-30 — "My sheep hear my voice, and I know them, and they follow me; and

	I give them eternal life, and they shall never perish, and no one shall snatch them out of my hand. My Father, who has given them to me, is greater than all, and no one is able to snatch them out of the Father's hand. I and the Father are one."
Revelation 1:8	"I am the Alpha and the Omega," says the Lord God, who is and who was and who is to come, the Almighty.
John 8:56-58	"Your father Abraham rejoiced that he was to see my day; he saw it and was glad." The Jews then said to him, "You are not yet fifty years old, and have you seen Abraham?" Jesus said to them, "Truly, truly, I say to you, before Abraham was, I am."

Bahá'í References

Know thou assuredly that the essence of all the Prophets of God is one and the same. Their unity is absolute. God, the Creator, saith: There is no distinction whatsoever among the Bearers of My Message. They all have but one purpose; their secret is the same secret. To prefer one in honor to another, to exalt certain ones above the rest, is in no wise to be permitted. Every true Prophet hath regarded His Message as fundamentally the same as the Revelation of every other Prophet gone before Him.

Bahá'u'lláh
Gleanings, pp. 78-79

These sanctified Mirrors, these Day Springs of ancient glory, are, one and all, the Exponents on earth of Him Who is the central Orb of the Universe, its Essence and ultimate Purpose. From Him proceed their knowledge and power; from Him is derived their sovereignty . . . . These Tabernacles of Holiness, these Primal Mirrors which reflect the light of unfading glory, are but expressions of Him Who is the Invisible of the Invisibles. By the revelation of these Gems of Divine virtue all the names and attributes of God, such as knowledge and power, sovereignty and dominion, mercy and wisdom, glory, bounty, and grace, are made manifest . . . . all the Prophets of God, His well-favored, His holy and chosen Messengers are, without exception, the bearers of His names, and the embodiments of His attributes. They only differ in the intensity of their revelation, and the comparative potency of their light.

Bahá'u'lláh
Gleanings, pp. 47-48

Beware, O believers in the Unity of God, lest ye be tempted to make any distinction between any of the

Manifestations of His Cause, or to discriminate against the signs that have accompanied and proclaimed their Revelation. This indeed is the true meaning of Divine Unity, if ye be of them that apprehend and believe this truth.

Bahá'u'lláh
Gleanings, p. 59

Thus He saith: "Our Cause is but one." Inasmuch as the Cause is one and the same, the Exponents thereof also must needs be one and the same.

Bahá'u'lláh
Kitáb-i-Iqán, p. 153

The Cause of Bahá'u'lláh is the same as the Cause of Christ. It is the same Temple and the same Foundation. Both of these are spiritual springtimes and seasons of the soul-refreshing awakening and the cause of the renovation of the life of mankind. The spring of this year is the same as the spring of last year. The origins and ends are the same. The sun of today is the sun of yesterday. In the coming of Christ, the divine teachings were given in accordance with the infancy of the human race. The teachings of Bahá'u'lláh have the same basic principles, but are according to the stage of the maturity of the world and the requirements of this illumined age.

'Abdu'l-Bahá
Bahá'í World Faith, p. 400

PART TWO:
SOME CHRISTIAN SUBJECTS

EARLY CHRISTIANS IN ROME
listening to a reading from the Scriptures.
(Romans 1:7)

THE WORD OF GOD

Jesus said: "Heaven and earth shall pass away; but my words shall not pass away." (Luke 21:33) However, Jesus is not the only "Word." The Words of God are endless.

Christians know and understand that the Word of God was revealed in stages. The earliest Hebrew prophets spoke to the people and gave them God's Word—Abraham, Noah, Jacob, and others. Then Moses appeared and spoke the Word of God, bringing a new Law. After him, the minor prophets of Israel continued to guide the people with the Word of God—Isaiah, Jeremiah, Ezekiel, and so forth. When Jesus Christ began His ministry, He represented the Word of God for His day.

Bahá'ís call this periodic dispensation of God's Will "progressive revelation." In every age, the Word of God is renewed with the appearance of a new prophet or Manifestation of God who brings the teachings which are needed in proportion to our stage of maturity. As Jesus said: "I have yet many things to say to you, but you cannot bear them now. When the Spirit of truth comes, he will guide you into all the truth . . ." Nonetheless, the spiritual truth of the Word of God is never changed. Only the presentation of the Word of God, the outward forms of religion, will change to suit the time and the place where they appear.

Biblical References

John 1:14   And the Word became flesh and dwelt among us, full of grace and truth . . .

John 3:31-36   He who comes from above is above all; he who is of the earth belongs to the earth, and of the earth he speaks; he who comes from heaven is above all. He bears witness to what he has seen and heard, yet no one receives his testimony; he who receives his testimony sets his seal to this, that God is true. For he whom God has sent utters the words of God, for it is not by measure that he gives the Spirit; the Father loves the Son, and has given all things into his hand. He who believes in the Son has eternal life . . .

John 3:12   "If I have told you earthly things and you do not believe, how can you believe if I tell you heavenly things?"

John 16:12   "I have yet many things to say to you, but you cannot bear them now. When the Spirit of truth comes, he will guide you into all the truth."

Bahá'í References

The Word of God is sanctified from time. The past, the present, the future, all, in relation to God, are equal. Yesterday, today, tomorrow do not exist in the sun.

In the same way there is priority with regard to glory—that is to say, the most glorious precedes the glorious. Therefore, the Reality of Christ, Who is the Word of God, with regard to essence, attributes and glory, certainly precedes the creatures. Before appearing in the human form, the Word of God was in the utmost sanctity and glory, existing in perfect beauty and splendor in the height of its magnificence. When through the wisdom of God the Most High it shone from the heights of glory in the world of the body, the Word of God, through this body, became oppressed, so that it fell into the hands of the Jews, and became the captive of the tyrannical and ignorant, and at last was crucified.

'Abdu'l-Bahá
Some Answered Questions, p. 116-17

Yet the Sun of Reality, the Word of God, shone from the Messianic mirror through the wonderful channel of Jesus Christ more fully and more wonderfully. Its effulgences were manifestly radiant, but even to this day the Jews are holding to the Mosaic mirror. Therefore, they are bereft of witnessing the lights of eternity in Jesus.

'Abdu'l-Bahá
Promulgation of Universal Peace, p. 115

There is no intrinsic meaning in the leaves of a book, but the thought they convey leads you to reflect upon reality. The reality of Jesus was the perfect meaning, the Christhood in Him which in the Holy Books is symbolized as the Word.

'Abdu'l-Bahá
Promulgation of Universal Peace, p. 155

"The Word was with God." The Christhood means not the body of Jesus but the perfection of divine virtues manifest in Him. Therefore, it is written, "He is God." This does not imply separation from God, even as it is not possible to separate the rays of the sun from the sun. The reality of Christ was the embodiment of divine virtues and attributes of God. For in Divinity there is no duality. All adjectives, nouns and pronouns in that court of sanctity are one; there is neither multiplicity nor division. The intention of this explanation is to show that the Words of God have innumerable significances and mysteries of meanings—each one a thousand and more.

'Abdu'l-Bahá
Promulgation of Universal Peace, p. 155

RETURN OF THE PRODIGAL SON
"His father saw him and had compassion, and ran and embraced him and kissed him." (Luke 15:20)

SALVATION!

Most Christians believe that Christ came to die on the cross for the remission of our sins, and that in Christ's martyrdom we can find our salvation. Of course, this is true—and this is the case with all the Manifestations of God—if our faith is supported by deeds. Not only Christ's sacrifice on the cross, but also His life and His teachings can enable us to overcome all sin, such as anger, hatred, prejudice, greed, selfishness, etc. However, if these sins cannot be overcome, then the sacrifice of Jesus on the cross is of no benefit to us. "So faith by itself, if it has no works, is dead." (James 2:17)

Biblical References

Matthew 7:21	"Not everyone who says to me, 'Lord, Lord,' shall enter the kingdom of heaven, but he who does the will of my Father who is in heaven."
Matthew 19:16-17	And behold, one came up to him, saying, "Teacher, what good deed

must I do, to have eternal life?" And he said to him, "Why do you ask me about what is good? One there is who is good. If you would enter life, keep the commandments."

James 2:14-17
What does it profit, my brethren, if a man says he has faith but has not works? Can his faith save him? If a brother or sister is ill-clad and in lack of daily food, and one of you says to them, "Go in peace, be warmed and filled," without giving them the things needed for the body, what does it profit? So faith by itself, if it has no works, is dead.

Bahá'í References

You ask if, through the appearance of the kingdom of God, every soul hath been saved. The Sun of Reality hath appeared to all the world. This luminous appearance is salvation and life; but only he who hath opened the eye of reality and who hath seen these lights will be saved.

'Abdu'l-Bahá
Bahá'í World Faith, pp. 389-90

He is Alpha and Omega. He is the One that will give unto him that is athirst of the fountain of the water of life and bestow upon the sick the remedy of true salvation. He whom such grace aideth is verily he that receiveth the most glorious heritage from the Prophets of God and His holy ones. The Lord will be his God, and he His dearly-loved son.

'Abdu'l-Bahá
Selections from the Writings of 'Abdu'l-Bahá, p. 13

When the sanctified breezes of Christ and the holy light of the Greatest Luminary were spread abroad, the human realities—that is to say, those who turned toward the Word of God and received the profusion of His bounties—were saved from this attachment and sin, obtained everlasting life, were delivered from the chains of bondage, and attained to the world of liberty. They were freed from the vices of the human world, and were blessed by the virtues of the Kingdom.

'Abdu'l-Bahá
Some Answered Questions, p. 125

The first duty prescribed by God for His servants is the recognition of Him Who is the Day Spring of His Revelation and the Fountain of His laws, Who representeth the Godhead in both the Kingdom of His Cause and the world of creation. Whoso achieveth this duty hath attained unto all good; and whoso is deprived thereof, hath gone astray, though he be the author of every righteous deed. It behooveth every one who reacheth this most sublime station, this summit of transcendent glory, to observe every ordinance of Him Who is the Desire of the world. These twin duties are inseparable. Neither is acceptable without the other. Thus hath it been decreed by Him Who is the Source of Divine Inspiration."

Bahá'u'lláh
Kitáb-i-Aqdas, p. 11

BAPTISM

Most Christian churches require baptism in water before one can be considered a true Christian. There are various customs and practices associated with baptism, and these have become an important part of church life. However, Bahá'ís believe that these ceremonies in themselves have no effect on the soul. Originally, baptism was intended to be a symbol of repentance and of the cleansing power of Christian belief. But the way that it is practiced today is quite different.

John the Baptist exhorted the people to repent. Only after they had done so did he baptize them—using water as a symbol of spiritual cleansing. Of course, the people that he baptized were Jews, and they remained Jews after baptism. John promised that Christ would baptize his followers with the Holy Spirit and with fire. Obviously, this baptism is symbolic, since baptism with spirit or with fire are physically impossible.

The ritual of baptism with water is not practiced in the Bahá'í Faith. But the need for a cleansing of the spirit and the renewal of one's inner life through religion is recognized and understood.

Biblical References

Matthew 3:11	"I baptize you with water for repentance, but he who is coming after me is mightier than I, whose sandals I am not worthy to carry; he will baptize you with the Holy Spirit and with fire."
John 1:29-33	The next day he saw Jesus coming toward him, and said, "Behold, the Lamb of God, who takes away the sin of the world! This is he of whom I said, 'After me comes a man who ranks before me, for he was before me.' I myself did not know him; . . . but he who sent me to baptize with water said to me, 'He on whom you see the Spirit descend and remain, this is he who baptizes with the Holy Spirit.'"
John 3:5-6	Jesus answered, "Truly, truly, I say to you, unless one is born of water and the Spirit, he cannot enter the kingdom of God. That which is born of the flesh is flesh, and that which is born of the Spirit is spirit."

Bahá'í References

The principle of baptism is purification by repentance. John admonished and exhorted the people, and caused them to repent; then he baptized them. Therefore, it is apparent that this baptism is a symbol of repentance from all sin: its meaning is expressed in these words: "O God! as my body has become purified and cleansed from physical impurities, in the same way purify and sanctify my spirit from the impurities of the world of nature, which are not worthy of the Threshold of Thy Unity!"

'Abdu'l-Bahá
Some Answered Questions, p. 91

As Christ desired that this institution of John should be used at that time by all, He Himself conformed to it in order to awaken the people and to complete the law of the former religion. Although the ablution of repentance was the institution of John, it was in reality formerly practiced in the religion of God.

Christ was not in need of baptism; but as at that time it was an acceptable and praiseworthy action, and a sign of the glad tidings of the Kingdom, therefore, He confirmed it. However, afterward He said the true baptism is not with material water, but it must be with spirit and with water. In this case water does not signify material water, for elsewhere it is explicitly said baptism is with spirit and with fire, from which it is clear that the reference is not to material fire and material water, for baptism with fire is impossible.

Therefore, the spirit is the bounty of God, the water is knowledge and life, and the fire is the love of God. For material water does not purify the heart of man; no, it cleanses his body. But the heavenly water and spirit, which are knowledge and life, make the human heart good and pure . . .

'Abdu'l-Bahá
Some Answered Questions, p. 91-92

Reflect, also, that baptism in the days of John the Baptist was used to awaken and admonish the people to repent from all sin, and to watch for the appearance of the Kingdom of Christ. But at present in Asia, the Catholics and the Orthodox Church plunge newly born children into water mixed with olive oil, and many of them become ill from the shock; at the time of baptism they struggle and become agitated. In other places, the clergy sprinkle the water of baptism on the forehead. But neither from the first form nor from the second do the children derive any spiritual benefit.

'Abdu'l-Bahá
Some Answered Questions, p. 94-95

THE LORD'S SUPPER

Holy Communion, or the sacrament of the Eucharist, is another practice that is observed by most Christian churches. Again, Bahá'ís see this ritual as symbolic, rather than having—in itself—any effect on the soul. When Christ said: "I am the bread of life; he who comes to me shall not hunger, and he who believes in me shall never thirst," (John 6:35) He was obviously talking in symbolic terms.

Biblical References

Matthew 26:26-29	Now as they were eating, Jesus took bread, and blessed, and broke it, and gave it to the disciples and said, "Take, eat; this is my body." And he took a cup, and when he had given thanks he gave it to them, saying, "Drink of it, all of you; for this is my blood of the covenant, which is poured out for many for the forgiveness of sins. I tell you I shall not drink again of this fruit of the vine

until that day when I drink it new with you in my Father's kingdom."

Mark 14:22-25

And as they were eating, he took bread, and blessed, and broke it, and gave it to them, and said, "Take; this is my body." And he took a cup, and when he had given thanks he gave it to them, and they all drank of it. And he said to them, "This is my blood of the covenant, which is poured out for many. Truly, I say to you, I shall not drink again of the fruit of the vine until that day when I drink it new in the kingdom of God."

Luke 22:17-20

And he took a cup, and when he had given thanks he said, "Take this, and divide it among yourselves; for I tell you that from now on I shall not drink of the fruit of the vine until the kingdom of God comes." And he took bread, and when he had given thanks he broke it and gave it to them, saying, "This is my body . . ."

John 6:47-63

"Truly, truly, I say to you, he who believes has eternal life. I am the bread of life. Your fathers ate the manna in the wilderness, and they died. This is the bread which comes

THE LORD'S SUPPER

down from heaven, that a man may eat of it and not die. I am the living bread which came down from heaven; if any one eats of this bread, he will live for ever; and the bread which I shall give for the life of the world is my flesh."

The Jews then disputed among themselves, saying, "How can this man give us his flesh to eat?" So Jesus said to them, "Truly, truly, I say to you unless you eat the flesh of the Son of man and drink his blood, you have no life in you; he who eats my flesh and drinks my blood has eternal life, and I will raise him up at the last day. For my flesh is food indeed, and my blood is drink indeed. He who eats my flesh and drinks my blood abides in me, and I in him. As the living Father sent me, and I live because of the Father, so he who eats me will live because of me. This is the bread which came down from heaven, not such as the fathers ate and died; he who eats this bread will live for ever." This he said in the synagogue, as he taught at Capernum.

Many of his disciples, when they heard it, said, "This is a hard saying; who can listen to it?" But Jesus, knowing in himself that his disciples murmured at it, said to them, "Do you take offense at this? Then what if you were to see the Son of man ascending where he was before? It is the spirit that gives life, the flesh is of no avail; the words that I have spoken to you are spirit and life."

John 6:33   "For the bread of God is that which comes down from heaven, and gives life to the world."

Bahá'í References

The position of Christ was that of absolute perfection; He made His divine perfections shine like the sun upon all believing souls, and the bounties of the light shone and radiated in the reality of men. This is why He says: "I am the bread which descended from heaven; whosoever shall eat of this bread will not die."—that is to say, that whosoever shall partake of this divine food will attain unto eternal life: that is, every one who partakes of this bounty and receives these perfections will find eternal life, will obtain preexistent favors, will be freed from the darkness of error, and will be illuminated by the light of His guidance.

'Abdu'l-Bahá
Some Answered Questions, p. 121

This is the meaning of the words of Christ, "I gave My blood for the life of the world"—that is to say, I have chosen all these troubles, these sufferings, calamities, and even the greatest martyrdom, to attain this object, the remission of sins (that is, the detachment of spirits from the human world, and their attraction to the divine world) in order that souls may arise who will be the very essence of the guidance of mankind, and the manifestations of the perfections of the Supreme Kingdom.

'Abdu'l-Bahá
Some Answered Questions, p. 121

Although they consider the wine and the bread in the church as the blood and body of Christ, yet this is but the appearance and not the reality. But the reality of Christ is the words of the Holy Spirit. If thou art able, take a portion thereof.

'Abdu'l-Bahá
Bahá'í World Faith, p. 390

The Supper of the Lord which His Highness the Spirit [Jesus] ate with the apostles was a heavenly supper and not one of material bread and water, for material objects have no connection with spiritual objects. As at that time material food was also present, therefore the leaders of the religion of Christ thought that it was material food which was changed into spiritual food.

The proof that it was not material food is this: The apostles upon many occasions partook of material food with His Highness Christ, yet the supper of that night became designated as the "Lord's Supper." From this designation it is plain and evident that they ate heavenly food at that supper. That heavenly food consisted of the love of God, the knowledge of God, the mysteries of God and the bestowal of God."

'Abdu'l-Bahá
Bahá'í World Faith, p. 390-91

Make ye an effort in every meeting that the Lord's Supper may become realized and the heavenly food descend. This heavenly food is knowledge, understanding, faith, assurance, love, affinity, kindness, purity of purpose, attraction of hearts and the union of souls. It was this manner of the Lord's Supper which descended from the heavenly kingdom in the day of Christ.

'Abdu'l-Bahá
Bahá'í World Faith, p. 407-408

RESURRECTION AND JUDGMENT DAY

All of the prophetic religions speak of a Day of Judgment or a Day of Resurrection. Although the scriptures speak extensively about this matter, it continues to be one of the most misunderstood questions in every religion. Although Jesus said, "I am the resurrection and the life," many Christians understand the Judgment Day to be the end of history, rather than the beginning of new life. They imagine grand apocalyptic scenes in which bodies come up from their graves, angels fly down from the sky and people are sent to a physical heaven or a physical hell.

For Bahá'ís, every divine Manifestation of God is the "resurrection" by which people are judged. Those who accept the Manifestation for their day have judged themselves. They are "resurrected" to new life by their choice.

Biblical References

John 11:25-26	Jesus said to her, "I am the resurrection and the life; he who believes in

me, though he die, yet shall he live, and whoever lives and believes in me shall never die. Do you believe this?"

John 9:39-41 Jesus said, "For judgment I came into this world, that those who do not see may see, and that those who see may become blind." Some of the Pharisees near him heard this, and they said to him, "Are we also blind?" Jesus said to them, "If you were blind, you would have no guilt; but now that you say, 'We see,' your guilt remains."

John 3:18-13 He who believes in him is not condemned; he who does not believe is condemned already, because he has not believed in the name of the only Son of God. And this is the judgment, that the light has come into the world, and men loved darkness rather than light, because their deeds were evil.

John 5:22-25 "The Father judges no one, but has given all judgment to the Son, that all may honor the Son, even as they honor the Father. He who does not honor the Son does not honor the

Father who sent him. Truly, truly, I say to you, he who hears my word and believes him who sent me, has eternal life; he does not come into judgment, but has passed from death to life."

John 12:30-31
Jesus answered, "This voice has come for your sake, not for mine. Now is the judgment of this world, now shall the ruler of this world be cast out . . ."

Bahá'í References

This is the Day whereon every man will fly from himself, how much more from his kindred, could ye but perceive it. Say: By God! The blast hath been blown on the trumpet, and lo, mankind hath swooned away before us! The Herald hath cried out, and the Summoner raised His voice saying: 'The Kingdom is God's, the Most Powerful, the Help in Peril, the Self-Subsisting.

Bahá'u'lláh
Gleanings, p. 43-44

. . . by "Resurrection" is meant the rise of the Manifestation of God to proclaim His Cause, and by "attainment unto the divine Presence" is meant attainment unto the presence of His Beauty in the person of His Manifestation.

Bahá'u'lláh
Kitáb-i-Iqán, p. 170

. . . what is meant by the Day of Resurrection is this, that from the time of the appearance of Him Who is the Tree of divine Reality, at whatever period and under whatever name, until the moment of His disappearance, is the Day of Resurrection. For example, from the inception of the mission of Jesus—may peace be upon Him—till the day of His ascension was the Resurrection of Moses. For during that period the Revelation of God shone forth through the appearance of that divine Reality, Who rewarded by His Word everyone who [believed in Moses, and punished by His Word everyone who] did not believe; inasmuch as God's Testimony for that Day was that which He had solemnly affirmed in the Gospel.

The Báb
*Selections from the
Writings of the Báb,* p. 106-07

Therefore, whosoever, and in whatever Dispensation, hath recognized and attained unto the presence of these glorious, these resplendent and most excellent Luminaries, hath verily attained unto the "Presence of God" Himself, and entered the city of eternal and immortal life. Attainment unto such presence is possible only in the Day of Resurrection, which is the Day of the rise of God Himself through His all-embracing Revelation.

This is the meaning of the "Day of Resurrection," spoken of in all of the scriptures, and announced unto all people.

Bahá'u'lláh
Kitáb-i-Iqán, p. 143

Strive, therefore, O my brother, to grasp the meaning of "Resurrection," and cleanse thine ears from the idle sayings of these rejected people. Shouldst thou step into the realm of complete detachment, thou wilt readily testify that no day is mightier than this Day, and that no resurrection more awful than this Resurrection can ever be conceived.

Bahá'u'lláh
Kitáb-i-Iqán, p. 144

THE MEANING OF "LIFE" AND "DEATH"

Many passages in the Holy Scriptures refer to the mystery of life and death. And these clearly differentiate between spiritual life and spiritual death, as opposed to physical life and physical death. The Bible, as well as the Bahá'í Scriptures, explains that spiritual life is the cause of eternal happiness—whereas physical life is, of course, only temporary.

The physical body lasts only a few decades, at most. It is the spiritual that is eternal. However, as physical beings, we may acquire spiritual attributes by directing our hearts to the light of Divine Guidance, by developing our latent talents, by service to our fellow human beings, by prayer and study of the Sacred Texts, and by facing the tests that this physical world provides. In these ways can we develop the life of the spirit. Otherwise, we are as dead—though we may be physically alive.

Biblical References

Matthew 8:21-22   Another of the disciples said to him, "Lord, let me first go and bury my father." But Jesus said to him, "Follow me, and leave the dead to bury their own dead."

Revelation 3:1-2 — "'I know your works; you have the name of being alive, and you are dead. Awake, and strengthen what remains and is on the point of death, for I have not found your works perfect in the sight of God.'"

John 5:25 — "Truly, truly, I say to you, the hour is coming, and now is, when the dead will hear the voice of the Son of God, and those who hear will live."

John 6:63 — "It is the spirit that gives life, the flesh is of no avail; the words that I have spoken to you are spirit and life."

John 11:25-26 — Jesus said to her, "I am the resurrection and the life; he who believes in me, though he die, yet shall he live, and whoever lives and believes in me shall never die."

I John 3:13-14 — Do not wonder, brethren, that the world hates you. We know that we have passed out of death into life, because we love the brethren. He who does not love abides in death.

LIFE AND DEATH

Bahá'í References

By the terms "life" and "death," spoken of in the scriptures, is intended the life of faith and the death of unbelief. The generality of the people, owing to their failure to grasp the meaning of these words, rejected and despised the person of the Manifestation, deprived themselves of the light of His divine guidance, and refused to follow the example of that immortal Beauty.

Bahá'u'lláh
Kitáb-i-Iqán, p. 114

... true life is not the life of the flesh but the life of the spirit. For the life of the flesh is common to both men and animals, whereas the life of the spirit is possessed only by the pure in heart who have quaffed from the ocean of faith and partaken of the fruit of certitude. This life knoweth no death, and this existence is crowned by immortality. Even as it hath been said: "He who is a true believer liveth both in this world and in the world to come." If by "life" be meant this earthly life, it is evident that death must needs overtake it.

Bahá'u'lláh
Kitáb-i-Iqán, p. 120-21

Observe: those who in appearance were physically alive, Christ considered dead; for life is the eternal life, and existence is the real existence. Wherever in the Holy Books they speak of raising the dead, the meaning is that the dead were blessed by eternal life; where it is said that the blind received sight, the signification is that he obtained the true perception; where it is said a deaf man received hearing, the meaning is that he acquired spiritual and heavenly hearing.

'Abdu'l-Bahá
Some Answered Questions, p. 101-102

That is why those who were heedless and denied God were said by Christ to be dead, although they were apparently living; in relation to the people of faith they were dead, blind, deaf and dumb. This is what Christ meant when said, "Let the dead bury their dead."

'Abdu'l-Bahá
Some Answered Questions, p. 279

Such things have come to pass in the days of every Manifestation of God. Even as Jesus said: "Ye must be born again." Again He saith: "Except a man be born of water and of the Spirit, he cannot enter into the Kingdom of God. That which is born of the flesh is flesh; and that which is born of the Spirit is spirit." The purport of these words is that whosoever in every dispensation is born of the Spirit and is quickened by the breath of the Manifestation of Holiness, he verily is of those that have attained unto "life" and "resurrection" and have entered into the "paradise" of the love of God. And whosoever is not of them, is condemned to "death" and "deprivation," to the "fire" of unbelief, and to the "wrath" of God.

Bahá'u'lláh
Kitáb-i-Iqán, p. 118

THE PARABLE OF THE VINEYARD
"... and the tenants took his servants and beat one, killed another, and stoned another." (Matthew 21:35)

THE SYMBOLIC MEANINGS OF PARABLES

Jesus told many parables which are recorded in the Bible. He used parables extensively to express—through metaphor and colorful imagery—certain spiritual concepts which otherwise would have been difficult or impossible to explain. The parables present spiritual truths through material imagery and example.

Taking parables literally is a serious mistake. It requires prayer, meditation, and careful study to uncover the spiritual verities which are found in the parables of Jesus. A literal understanding of these stories is always misleading.

Many of these parables concern the "Kingdom of God." Meditation on these parables can open the doors of God's Kingdom to the sincere seeker. Jesus uses these parables to talk about the time of His coming—and to talk about the coming of the Promised One. In the Parable of the Vineyard, the Parable of the Marriage Feast, and the Parable of the Ten Maidens, Jesus explains in symbolic terms the nature of the coming of any Manifestation of God and how He is received by the careless and the faithful.

Biblical References

Matthew 13:34-35	All this Jesus said to the crowds in parables; indeed he said nothing to them without a parable. This was to fulfill what was spoken by the prophet: "I will open my mouth in parables, I will utter what has been hidden since the foundation of the world."
Mark 4:10-12	And when he was alone, those who were about him with the twelve asked him concerning the parables. And he said to them, "To you has been given the secret of the kingdom of God, but for those outside everything is in parables; so that they may indeed see but not perceive, and may indeed hear but not understand; lest they should turn again, and be forgiven."
Luke 8:9-10	And when his disciples asked him what this parable meant, he said, "To you has been given to know the secrets of the kingdom of God; but for others they are in parables, so that seeing they may not see, and hearing they may not understand."

PARABLES

Mark 4:33-34

With many such parables he spoke the word to them, as they were able to hear it; he did not speak to them without a parable, but privately to his own disciples he explained everything.

Matthew 13:10-15

Then the disciples came and said to him, "Why do you speak to them in parables?" And he answered them, "To you it has been given to know the secrets of the kingdom of heaven, but to them it has not been given. For to him who has will more be given, and he will have abundance; but from him who has not, even what he has will be taken away. This is why I speak to them in parables, because seeing they do not see, and hearing they do not hear, nor do they understand. With them indeed is fulfilled the prophecy of Isaiah which says:
 'You shall indeed hear but never understand,
 and you shall indeed see but never perceive.'"

Matthew 22:1-14

And again Jesus spoke to them in parables, saying, "The kingdom of heaven may be compared to a king who gave a marriage feast for his son, and sent his servants to call those who were invited to the marriage feast; but they would not come. Again he sent other servants, saying, 'Tell those who are invited, Behold, I have made ready my dinner, my oxen and my fat calves are killed, and everything is ready; come to the marriage feast.' But they made light of it and went off, one to his farm, another to his business, while the rest seized his servants, treated them shamefully, and killed them. The king was angry, and he sent his troops and destroyed those murderers and burned their city. Then he said to his servants, 'The wedding is ready, but those invited were not worthy. Go therefore to the thoroughfares, and invite to the marriage feast as many as you find.' And those servants went out into the streets and gathered all whom they found, both bad and good; so the wedding hall was filled with guests.

"But when the king came in to look at the guests, he saw there a man who had no wedding garment; and he said to him, 'Friend, how did you get in here without a wedding garment!' And he was speechless. Then the king said to the attendants, 'Bind him hand and foot, and cast him into the outer darkness; there men will weep and gnash their teeth.' For many are called, but few are chosen."

Matthew 25:1-13

"Then the kingdom of heaven shall be compared to ten maidens who took their lamps and went to meet the bridegroom. Five of them were foolish, and five were wise. For when the foolish took their lamps, they took no oil with them; but the wise took flasks of oil with their lamps. As the bridegroom was delayed, they all slumbered and slept. But at midnight there was a cry, 'Behold, the bridegroom! Come out to meet him.' Then all those maidens rose and trimmed their lamps. And the foolish said to the wise, 'Give us some of your oil, for our lamps are going out.' But the wise replied, 'Perhaps there will not be enough for us and for you; go rather to the dealers and buy for yourselves.' And while they went to buy, the bridegroom came, and those who were ready went in with him to the marriage feast; and the door was shut. Afterward the other maidens came also, saying, 'Lord, lord, open to us.'

But he replied, 'Truly, I say to you, I do not know you.' Watch therefore, for you know neither the day nor the hour."

Matthew 21:33-43

"Hear another parable. There was a householder who planted a vineyard, and set a hedge around it, and dug a wine press in it, and built a tower, and let it out to tenants, and went into another country. When the season of fruit drew near, he sent his servants to the tenants, to get his fruit; and the tenants took his servants and beat one, killed another, and stoned another. Again he sent other servants, more than the first; and they did the same to them. Afterward he sent his son to them, saying, 'They will respect my son.' But when the tenants saw the son, they said to themselves, 'This is the heir; come, let us kill him and have his inheritance.' And they took him and cast him out of the vineyard, and killed him. When therefore the owner of the vineyard comes, what will he do to those tenants?" They said to him, "He will put those wretches to a miserable death, and let out the vineyard to other tenants who will give him the fruits in their seasons."

Jesus said to them, "Have you never read in the scriptures:
'The very stone which the builders rejected
has become the head of the corner;
this was the Lord's doing,
and it is marvelous in our eyes'?
Therefore I tell you, the kingdom of God will be taken away from you and given to a nation producing the fruits of it."

Bahá'í References

Lo! The Father is come, and that which ye were promised in the Kingdom is fulfilled! This is the Word which the Son concealed, when to those around Him He said: "Ye cannot bear it now." And when the appointed time was fulfilled and the Hour had struck, the Word shone forth above the horizon of the Will of God. Beware, O followers of the Son, that ye cast it not behind your backs.

Bahá'u'lláh
Tablets of Bahá'u'lláh, p. 11

You are like unto the man who layeth out an orchard and planteth all kinds of fruit trees therein. When the time is at hand for him, the lord, to come, ye will have taken possession of the orchard in his name, and when he doth come in person, ye will shut him out from it.

Verily We planted the Tree . . . and provided its Orchard with all kinds of fruit, whereof ye all have been partaking. Then when We came to take over that which We had planted, ye pretended not to know Him Who is the Lord thereof.

Be ye not a cause of grief unto Us, nor withhold Us from this Orchard which belongeth unto Us, though independent are We of all that ye possess. . . .

We have planted the Garden of the Bayán in the name of Him Whom God will make manifest (i.e., Bahá'u'lláh), and have granted you permission to live therein until the time of His manifestation; then from the moment the Cause of Him Whom God will make manifest is inaugurated, We forbid you all the things ye hold as your own, unless ye may, by the leave of your Lord, be able to regain possession thereof.

The Báb
*Selections from the
Writings of the Báb,* p. 135

THE MISSION OF CHRIST

Jesus explained that He was sent to the people in order to teach them about the Kingdom of God. The mission of Christ was the same as the mission of all the Manifestations of God: they each came at a particular time in history to bring us the Divine Teachings and to prepare the way for the Day promised to all mankind.

Jesus came to humanity as a Divine Teacher, to free us from the vices and sins of attachment to this world and to attract us to the Word of God. Those who believed in Him and followed His teachings were saved. They passed from death to life.

Biblical References

Luke 4:42-43	And when it was day he departed and went into a lonely place. And the people sought him and came to him, and would have kept him from leaving them; but he said to them, "I must preach the good news of the

	kingdom of God to the other cities also; for I was sent for this purpose."
John 18:37	Pilate said to him, "So you are a king?" Jesus answered, "You say that I am a king. For this I was born, and for this I have come into the world, to bear witness to the truth."
Matthew 10:34	"Do not think that I have come to bring peace on earth; I have not come to bring peace, but a sword."
John 11:25-26	"I am the resurrection and the life; he who believes in me, though he die, yet shall he live, and whoever lives and believes in me shall never die."

Bahá'í References

... is not the object of every Revelation to effect a transformation in the whole character of mankind, a transformation that shall manifest itself both outwardly and inwardly, that shall affect both its inner life and external conditions? For if the character of mankind be not changed, the futility of God's universal Manifestations would be apparent.

Bahá'u'lláh
Kitáb-i-Iqán, p. 240-241

Jesus Christ came to teach the people of the world this heavenly civilization and not material civilization. He breathed the breath of the Holy Spirit into the body of the world and established an illumined civilization. Among the principles of divine civilization He came to proclaim is the Most Great Peace of mankind. Among His principles of spiritual civilization is the oneness of the kingdom of humanity. Among the principles of heavenly civilization He brought is the virtue of the human world. Among the principles of celestial civilization He announced is the improvement and betterment of human morals.

'Abdu'l-Bahá
Promulgation of Universal Peace, p. 11

Christ appeared in this world nineteen hundred years ago to establish ties of unity and bonds of love between the various nations and different communities. He cemented together the sciences of Rome and the splendors of the civilization of Greece. He also accomplished affiliation between the Assyrian kingdom and the power of Egypt. The blending of these nations in unity, love and agreement had been impossible, but Christ through divine power established this condition among the children of men.

'Abdu'l-Bahá
Promulgation of Universal Peace, p. 18

Jesus Christ was an Educator of humanity. His teachings were altruistic; His bestowal, universal.

He taught mankind by the power of the Holy Spirit and not through agency, for the human power is limited, whereas the divine power is illimitable and infinite. The influence and accomplishment of Christ will attest this.

'Abdu'l-Bahá
Promulgation of Universal Peace, p. 85

This young Man, Christ, by the help of a supernatural power, abrogated the ancient Mosaic Law, reformed the general morals, and once again laid the foundation of eternal glory for the Israelites. Moreover, He brought to humanity the glad tidings of universal peace, and spread abroad teachings which were not for Israel alone but were for the general happiness of the whole human race.

'Abdu'l-Bahá
Some Answered Questions, p. 16

When the sanctified breezes of Christ and the holy light of the Greatest Luminary [Bahah'u'llah] were spread abroad, the human realities—that is to say, those who turned toward the Word of God and received the profusion of His bounties—were saved from this attachment and sin, obtained everlasting life, were delivered from the chains of bondage, and attained to the world of liberty. They were freed from the vices of the human world, and were blessed by the virtues of the Kingdom. This is the meaning of the words of Christ, "I gave My blood for the life of the world"—that is to say, I have chosen all these troubles, these sufferings, calamities, and even the greatest martyrdom, to attain this object, the remission of sins (that is, the detachment of spirits from the human world, and their attraction to the divine world) in order that souls may arise who will be the very essence of the guidance of mankind, and the manifestations of the perfections of the Supreme Kingdom.

'Abdu'l-Bahá
Some Answered Questions, p. 125

FEEDING THE MULTITUDE
"How is it that you fail to perceive that I did not speak about bread?"
(Matthew 16:11)

THE MIRACLES OF CHRIST

Most of the miracles mentioned in the Holy Bible have an inner spiritual significance which goes beyond their outward form. Of course, it is not beyond the power of an omnipotent God to raise the dead, for instance, or to cure a leper of his disease. But, the prophets of God do not come into the world to provide a sideshow of miracles to entertain the crowd. The prophets come to teach spiritual truths that will influence the souls of all people.

If Christ raised bodies from the dead, as is recorded in the Gospels, of what real significance is this? Did not these same persons who were raised die again at some later date? Similarly, if the blind were given sight, the deaf hearing, and the lame made to walk, were these physical miracles not also only temporary?

But when the spiritually dead were given eternal life through Christ's words, or the spiritually blind were given permanent sight by His teaching, wasn't that the true and lasting miracle? Isn't that the miracle that we can experience today?

Biblical References

John
9:39-41

Jesus said, "For judgment I came into this world, that those who do not see may see, and that those who see may become blind." Some of the Pharisees near him heard this, and they said to him, "Are we also blind?" Jesus said to them,"If you were blind, you would have no guilt; but now that you say, 'We see,' your guilt remains."

Matthew
16: 8-12

But Jesus . . . said, "O men of little faith, why do you discuss among yourselves the fact that you have no bread? Do you not yet perceive? Do you not remember the five loaves of the five thousand, and how many baskets you gathered? . . . How is it that you fail to perceive that I did not speak about bread? Beware of the leaven of the Pharisees and Sadducees." Then they understood that he did not tell them to beware of the leaven of bread, but of the teaching of the Pharisees and Sadducees.

Luke
7:20-23

And when the men had come to him, they said, "John the Baptist has sent us to you saying, 'Are you he who is to come, or shall we look for another?'" In that hour he cured many of diseases and plagues and evil spirits, and on many that were blind he bestowed sight. And he answered them, "Go tell John what you have seen and heard: the blind receive their sight, the lame walk, lepers are cleansed, and the deaf hear, the dead are raised up, the poor have good news preached to them. And blessed is he who takes no offense at me."

Bahá'í References

... most of the miracles of the Prophets which are mentioned have an inner significance.
'Abdu'l-Bahá
Some Answered Questions, p. 37

I do not wish to mention the miracles of Bahá'u'lláh, for it may perhaps be said that these are traditions, liable both to truth and to error, like the accounts of the miracles of Christ in the Gospel, which come to us from the apostles, and not from anyone else, and are denied by the Jews.
'Abdu'l-Bahá
Some Answered Questions, p. 37

The meaning is not that the Manifestations are unable to perform miracles, for They have all power.

But for Them inner sight, spiritual healing and eternal life are the valuable and important things. Consequently, whenever it is recorded in the Holy Books that such a one was blind and recovered his sight, the meaning is that he was inwardly blind, and that he obtained spiritual vision, or that he was ignorant and became wise, or that he was negligent and became heedful, or that he was worldly and became heavenly.

'Abdu'l-Bahá
Some Answered Questions, p. 102

The Holy Manifestations are the sources of miracles and the originators of wonderful signs. For Them, any difficult and impracticable thing is possible and easy. For through a supernatural power wonders appear from Them; and by this power, which is beyond nature, They influence the world of nature. From all the Manifestations marvelous things have appeared.

'Abdu'l-Bahá
Some Answered Questions, p. 100

... if we relate to a seeker, a stranger to Moses and Christ, marvelous signs, he will deny them and will say: "Wonderful signs are also continually related of false gods by the testimony of many people, and they are affirmed in the Books. The Brahmans have written a book about wonderful prodigies from Brahma." He will also say: "How can we know that the Jews and the Christians speak the truth, and that the Brahmans tell a lie?" . . . Therefore, miracles are not a proof. For if they are proofs for those who are present, they fail as proofs to those who are absent.

'Abdu'l-Bahá
Some Answered Questions, pp. 100-101

Recollect that Christ, solitary and alone, without a helper or protector, without armies and legions, and under the greatest oppression, uplifted the standard of God before all the people of the world, and withstood them, and finally conquered all, although outwardly He was crucified. Now this is a veritable miracle which can never be denied. There is no need of any other proof of the truth of Christ.

'Abdu'l-Bahá
Some Answered Questions, p. 101

THE APOSTLES PREACHING THE GOSPEL

THE ASCENSION OF CHRIST

Jesus said, "No one has ascended into heaven but he who descended from heaven, the Son of man."(John 3:13) The physical body of Christ did not descend from heaven, but was born from the womb of His mother. It was the holy and divine Spirit of Jesus Christ that came down from heaven. His ascension was also spiritual.

Crucifying Jesus, His enemies believed that they had destroyed Him and that His teachings would vanish. They counted His death as a victory, yet in reality His Spirit was never touched. And that Spirit revived the disciples and conquered the world. Jesus had said, "It is the spirit that gives life, the flesh is of no avail; the words that I have spoken to you are spirit and life." (John 6:63)

Some of the resurrection stories in the Bible explain that the disciples, after the crucifixion of Christ, were sad and discouraged. Only after speaking about Jesus for the whole day, and going over the prophecies and scriptures concerning the Messiah, and breaking bread together did they realize that Jesus was alive in spirit and had been walking with them all along.

Biblical References

John 3:13 "No one has ascended into heaven but he who descended from heaven, the Son of man."

Luke 24:13-31 That very day two of them were going to a village named Emmaus, about seven miles from Jerusalem, and talking with each other about all these things that had happened. While they were talking and discussing together, Jesus himself drew near and went with them. But their eyes were kept from recognizing him. And he said to them, "What is this conversation which you are holding with each other as you walk?" And they stood still, looking sad. Then one of them named Cleopas, answered him, "Are you only a visitor to Jerusalem who does not know the things that have happened there in these days?" And he said to them, "What things?" And they said to him, "Concerning Jesus of Nazareth, who was a prophet mighty in deed and word before God and all the people, and how our chief priests and rulers delivered him up to be condemned to death, and crucified him. But we had hoped that he was the one to redeem Israel. Yes, and besides all this, it is now the third day since this happened. Moreover, some women of our company amazed us. They were at the tomb early in the morning and did not find his body; and they came back saying that they had even seen a vision of angels, who said that he was alive. Some of those who were with us went to the tomb, and found it just as the women had said; but him they did not see." And he said to them, "O foolish men, and slow of heart to believe all that the prophets have spoken! Was it not necessary that the Christ should suffer these things and enter into his glory?" And beginning with Moses and all the prophets, he interpreted to them in all the scriptures the things concerning himself.

So they drew near to the village to which they were going. He appeared to be going further, but they constrained him, saying, "Stay with us, for it is toward evening and the day is now far spent." So he went in to stay with them. When he was at table with them, he took the bread and blessed, and broke it, and gave it to them. And their eyes were opened and they recognized him; and he vanished out of their sight.

Bahá'í References

The resurrections of the Divine Manifestations are not of the body. All Their states, Their conditions, Their acts, the things They have established, Their teachings, Their expressions, Their parables and Their instructions have a spiritual and divine signification, and have no connection with material things.
'Abdu'l-Bahá
Some Answered Questions, p. 103

And as it has become evident that Christ came from the spiritual heaven of the Divine Kingdom, therefore, His disappearance under the earth for three days has an inner signification and is not an outward fact. In the same way, His resurrection from the interior of the earth is also symbolical; it is a spiritual and divine fact, and not material; and likewise His ascension to heaven is a spiritual and not material ascension.
'Abdu'l-Bahá
Some Answered Questions, p. 104

Therefore, we say that the meaning of Christ's resurrection is as follows: the disciples were troubled and agitated after the martyrdom of Christ. The Reality of Christ, which signifies His teachings, His bounties, His perfections and His spiritual power, was hidden and concealed for two or three days after His martyrdom, and was not resplendent and manifest. No, rather it was lost, for the believers were few in number and were troubled and agitated. The Cause of Christ was like a lifeless body; and when after three days the disciples became assured and steadfast, and began to serve the Cause of Christ, and resolved to spread the divine teachings, putting His counsels into practice, and arising to serve Him, the Reality of Christ became resplendent and His bounty appeared; His religion found life; His teachings and His admonitions became evident and visible. In other words, the Cause of Christ was like a lifeless body until the life and the bounty of the Holy Spirit surrounded it.

'Abdu'l-Bahá
Some Answered Questions, p. 104

Such is the meaning of the resurrection of Christ, and this was a true resurrection. But as the clergy have neither understood the meaning of the Gospels nor comprehended the symbols, therefore, it has been said that religion is in contradiction to science, and science in opposition to religion, as, for example, this subject of the ascension of Christ with an elemental body to the visible heaven is contrary to the science of mathematics. But when the truth of this subject becomes clear, and the symbol is explained, science in no way contradicts it; but, on the contrary, science and the intelligence affirm it.

'Abdu'l-Bahá
Some Answered Questions, pp. 104-105

. . . there is the subject of Christ's coming from heaven: it is clearly stated in many places in the Gospel that the Son of man came from heaven, He is in heaven, and He will go to heaven. So in chapter 6, verse 38, of the Gospel of John it is written: "For I came down from heaven"; and also in verse 42 we find: "And they said, Is not this Jesus, the son of Joseph, whose father and mother we know? how is it then that he saith, I came down from heaven?" Also in John, chapter 3, verse 13: "And no man hath ascended up to heaven, but He that came down from heaven, even the Son of man which is in heaven."

'Abdu'l-Bahá
Some Answered Questions, p. 103

Verily the heaven into which the Messiah rose up was not this unending sky, rather was His heaven the Kingdom of His beneficent Lord. Even as He Himself hath said, "I came down from heaven," and again, "The Son of Man is in heaven." Hence it is clear that His heaven is beyond all directional points; it encircleth all existence, and is raised up for those who worship God. Beg and implore thy Lord to lift thee up into that heaven, and give thee to eat of its food, in this age of majesty and might.

'Abdu'l-Bahá
*Selections from the
Writings of 'Abdu'l-Bahá*, pp. 167-68

THE ANNUNCIATION
"And behold, you will conceive in your womb and bear a son . . ."
(Luke 1:31)

JESUS, THE SON OF GOD

In many passages, the Bible refers to Jesus as the "Son of man" or the "Son of God." In the Bahá'í Writings, He is titled the "Spirit of God," the "Son of God," the "Son of man," and the "Essence of the Spirit."

The title "Son of God" does not mean that God, the All-Glorious, impregnated Mary and produced a physical son—since God is not a physical being and is far exalted above any human attribute. Rather, the term "Son of God" has a spiritual meaning. Similarly, other appellations have been given to other Manifestations of God: Moses was known as the Interlocutor, He Who spoke with God; Muhammad was known as the Friend of God, or the Apostle of God; Bahá'u'lláh took the title the "Glory of God."

Furthermore, Jesus conferred the title of "sons of God" on all those who believe in Him. (John 1:12-14) He explained that He and God were one in a figurative sense. For He was given the authority of God, and whoever accepted Him accepted God, whoever rejected Him rejected God.

Biblical References

John 10:27-30	"My sheep hear my voice, and I know them, and they follow me; and I give them eternal life, and they shall never perish, and no one shall snatch them out of my hand. My Father, who has given them to me, is greater than all, and no one is able to snatch them out of the Father's hand. I and the Father are one."
John 17:20-23	"I do not pray for these only, but also for those who believe in me through their word, that they may all be one; even as thou, Father, art in me, and I in thee, that they also may be in us, so that the world may believe that thou hast sent me. The glory which thou hast given me I have given to them, that they may be one even as we are one, I in them and thou in me, that they may become perfectly one . . ."
John 10:33-36	The Jews answered him, "It is not for a good work that we stone you but for blasphemy; because you, being a man, make yourself God." Jesus answered them, "Is it not written in your law, 'I said, you are

gods'? If he called them gods to whom the word of God came (and scripture cannot be broken) do you say of him whom the Father consecrated and sent into the world, 'You are blaspheming,' because I said, 'I am the Son of God'?"

John 5:19 Jesus said to them, "Truly, truly, I say to you, the Son can do nothing of his own accord, but only what he sees the Father doing . . ."

John 5:23 He who does not honor the Son does not honor the Father who sent him.

Bahá'í References

As to the position of Christianity, let it be stated without any hesitation or equivocation that its divine origin is unconditionally acknowledged, that the Sonship and Divinity of Jesus Christ are fearlessly asserted, that the divine inspiration of the Gospel is full recognized, that the reality of the mystery of the Immaculacy of the Virgin Mary is confessed, and the primacy of Peter, the Prince of the Apostles, is upheld and defended. The Founder of the Christian Faith is designated by Bahá'u'lláh as the *"Spirit of God,"* is proclaimed as the One Who *"appeared out of the breath of the Holy*

Ghost," and is even extolled as the *"Essence of the Spirit."* His mother is described as that *"veiled and immortal, that most beauteous, countenance,"* and the station of her Son eulogized as a *"station which hath been exalted above the imaginings of all that dwell on earth,"* whilst Peter is recognized as one who God has caused *"the mysteries of wisdom and of utterance to flow out of his mouth."* *"Know thou,"* Bahá'u'lláh has moreover testified, *"that when the Son of Man yielded up His breath to God, the whole creation wept with a great weeping. By sacrificing Himself, however, a fresh capacity was infused into all created things."*

Shoghi Effendi
Promised Day is Come, pp. 109-110

Jesus said unto him "Arise from thy bed; thy sins are forgiven thee." Certain Jews, standing by, protested saying: "Who can forgive sins, but God alone?" And immediately He perceived their thoughts, Jesus answering said unto them: "Whether it is easier to say to the sick of the palsy, arise, and take up thy bed, and walk; or to say, thy sins are forgiven thee? that ye may know that the Son of Man hath power on earth to forgive sins." This is the real sovereignty, and such is the power of God's chosen Ones!

Bahá'u'lláh
Kitáb-i-Iqán, pp. 133-134

When for the second time the unmistakable signs of Israel's disintegration, abasement, subjection and annihilation had become apparent, then the sweet and holy breathings of the Spirit of God (Jesus) were shed across Jordan and the land of Galilee; the cloud of Divine pity overspread those skies, and rained down the copious waters of the spirit, and after those swelling showers that came from the most great Sea, the Holy Land put forth its perfume and blossomed with the knowledge of God.

'Abdu'l-Bahá,
Secret of Divine Civilization, p. 80

Such were the words uttered by Christ. On account of these words they cavilled at and assailed Him when He said unto them, "Verily the Son is in the Father, and the Father is in the Son." Be thou informed of this, and learn thou the secrets of thy Lord. As for the deniers, they are veiled from God: they see not, they hear not, neither do they understand.

'Abdu'l-Bahá
*Selections from the
Writings of 'Abdu'l-Bahá,* pp. 42-43

Observe how those souls who drank the living waters of redemption at that gracious hands of Jesus, the Spirit of God, and came into the sheltering shade of the Gospel, attained to such a high plane of moral conduct that Galen, the celebrated physician, although not himself a Christian, in his summary of Plato's Republic extolled their actions.

'Abdu'l-Bahá,
Secret of Divine Civilization, p. 84

Afterward Christ came, saying, "I am born of the Holy Spirit." Though it is now easy for the Christians to believe this assertion, at that time it was very difficult. According to the text of the Gospel the Pharisees said, "Is not this the son of Joseph of Nazareth Whom we know? How can He say, therefore, I came down from heaven."

'Abdu'l-Bahá,
Some Answered Questions, p. 16

WAS JESUS THE ONLY ONE WHO HAD NO FATHER?

Bahá'ís believe that Jesus was born into this world without a father. However, arguments over this issue are futile. The greatness of Christ does not depend on whether or not he had a physical father. The greatness of Christ rests on His life and His teachings. He was a Manifestation of God who, like all other Divine Teachers, demonstrated all perfections and glory.

We should note that Jesus is not the only one that the Bible states was born without a father. The Book of Hebrews indicates that "Melchizedek, king of Salem" was without father or mother. (Hebrews 7:1-3) Also, Adam—according to the Bible—was created by God without father or mother. And Eve, who became Adam's wife, was also created without parents. (Genesis 1:27 and 2:7, 21-22)

Biblical References

Matthew 1:18-25	Now the birth of Jesus Christ took place in this way. When his mother Mary had been betrothed to Joseph,

before they came together she was found to be with child of the Holy Spirit; and her husband Joseph, being a just man and unwilling to put her to shame, resolved to divorce her quietly. But as he considered this, behold, an angel of the Lord appeared to him in a dream, saying, "Joseph, son of David, do not fear to take Mary your wife, for that which is conceived in her is of the Holy Spirit; she will bear a son, and you shall call his name Jesus, for he will save his people from their sins." All this took place to fulfill what the Lord had spoken by the prophet:
"Behold, a virgin shall conceive and
  bear a son,
 and his name shall be called
  Emmanu-el"
(which means, God with us). When Joseph woke from sleep, he did as the angel of the Lord commanded him; he took his wife, but knew her not until she had borne a son; and he called his name Jesus.

John 6:41-42

The Jews then murmured at him, because he said, "I am the bread which came down from heaven." They said, "Is not this Jesus, the son of Joseph, whose father and mother we know? How does he now say, 'I have come down from heaven'?"

Bahá'í References

Likewise, reflect upon the state and condition of Mary. So deep was the perplexity of that most beauteous countenance, so grievous her case, that she bitterly regretted she had ever been born. To this beareth witness the text of the sacred verse wherein it is mentioned that after Mary had given birth to Jesus, she bemoaned her plight and cried out: "O would that I had died ere this, and been a thing forgotten, forgotten quite!" I swear by God! Such lamenting consumeth the heart and shaketh the being. Such consternation of the soul, such despondency, could have been caused by no other than the censure of the enemy and the cavilings of the infidel and perverse. Reflect, what answer could Mary have given to the people around her? How could she claim that a Babe Whose father was unknown had been conceived of the Holy Ghost? Therefore did Mary, that veiled and immortal Countenance, take up her Child and return unto her home. No sooner had the eyes of the people fallen upon her than they raised their voice saying: "O sister of Aaron! Thy father was not a man of wickedness, nor unchaste thy mother."

Bahá'u'lláh
Kitáb-i-Iqán, pp. 56-57

And now, meditate upon this most great convulsion, this grievous test. Notwithstanding all these things, God conferred upon that essence of the Spirit, Who was known amongst the people as fatherless, the glory of Prophethood, and made Him His testimony unto all that are in heaven and on earth.

Bahá'u'lláh
Kitáb-i-Iqán, p. 57

The honor and greatness of Christ is not due to the fact that He did not have a human father, but to His perfections, bounties and divine glory. If the greatness of Christ is His being fatherless, then Adam is greater than Christ, for He had neither father nor mother. It is said in the Old Testament, "And the Lord God formed man of the dust of the ground, and breathed into his nostrils the breath of life; and man became a living soul." Observe that it is said that Adam came into existence from the Spirit of life. Moreover, the expression which John uses in regard to the disciples proves that they also are from the Heavenly Father. Hence it is evident that the holy reality, meaning the real existence of every great man, comes from God and owes its being to the breath of the Holy Spirit.

The purport is that, if to be without a father is the greatest human glory, then Adam is greater than all, for He had neither father nor mother.

'Abdu'l-Bahá
Some Answered Questions, pp. 89-90

NO FATHER?

Then surely the first man had neither father nor mother, for the existence of man is phenomenal. Is not the creation of man without father and mother, even though gradually, more difficult than if he had simply come into existence without a father? As you admit that the first man came into existence without father or mother—whether it be gradually or at once—there can remain no doubt that a man without a human father is also possible and admissible; you cannot consider this impossible; otherwise you are illogical. For example, if you say that this lamp has once been lighted without wick and oil, and then say that it is impossible to light it without the wick, this is illogical." Christ had a mother; the first man, as the materialists believe, had neither father nor mother.

'Abdu'l-Bahá
Some Answered Questions, p. 88

JUDAS RECEIVING HIS PAYMENT
"And from that moment he sought an opportunity to betray him."
(Matthew 26:16)

THE MEANING OF ANTI-CHRIST

What is the anti-Christ? According to the Bible, any person or spirit that does not believe in Jesus Christ, does not glorify Him, and does not follow His teachings, that is anti-Christ. The Scriptures do not specify a certain time or place when the anti-Christ is to appear. John wrote that the anti-Christ was "in the world already." (1st John 4:3)

Of course, the Bahá'í Writings acknowledge the divinity of Jesus Christ and glorify Him. As to the anti-Christ, 'Abdu'l-Bahá explains that "wherever hatred and antagonism take the place of love and spiritual fellowship, Antichrist reigns instead of Christ."

Biblical References

1st John 2:22	Who is the liar but he who denies that Jesus is the Christ? This is the antichrist, he who denies the Father and the Son.
1st John 4:1-3	Beloved, do not believe every spirit, but test the spirits to see whether they

are of God; for many false prophets have gone out into the world. By this you know the Spirit of God: every spirit which confesses that Jesus Christ has come in the flesh is of God, and every spirit which does not confess Jesus is not of God. This is the spirit of antichrist, of which you heard that it was coming, and now it is in the world already.

Matthew 24:23-24 "Then if any one says to you, 'Lo, here is the Christ!' or 'There he is!' do not believe it. For false Christs and false prophets will arise and show great signs and wonders, so as to lead astray, if possible, even the elect."

Bahá'í References

Consider the sad picture of Italy carrying war into Tripoli. If you should announce that Italy was a barbarous nation and not Christian, this would be vehemently denied. But would Christ sanction what they are doing in Tripoli? Is this destruction of human life obedience to His laws and teachings? Where does He command it? Where does He consent to it? He was killed by His enemies; He did not kill. He even loved and prayed for those who hung Him on the cross. Therefore, these wars and cruelties, this bloodshed and sorrow are Antichrist, not Christ.

'Abdu'l-Bahá
The Promulgation of Universal Peace, p. 6

No less bitter is the conflict between sects and denominations. Christ was a divine Center of unity and love. Whenever discord prevails instead of unity, whenever hatred and antagonism take the place of love and spiritual fellowship, Antichrist reigns instead of Christ. Who is right in these controversies and hatreds between sects? . . . to be a Christian is not merely to bear the name of Christ and say, "I belong to a Christian government." To be a real Christian is to be a servant in His Cause and Kingdom, to go forth under His banner of peace and love toward all mankind . . .

'Abdu'l-Bahá
The Promulgation of Universal Peace, p. 6

PART THREE: THE PLAN OF GOD

THE MARTYRDOM OF STEPHEN
"Then they cast him out of the city and stoned him."
(Acts 7:58)

OPPOSITION TO THE PROPHETS OF GOD

Opposition to the Word of God can be found in the early history of all religions. There has never been a time when the majority of people have accepted the new teachings of any Manifestation of God with open arms. All of the Messengers of God have had to suffer because of the ignorance, corruption, wickedness, and opposition of their enemies.

Biblical References

Matthew 23:37	"O Jerusalem, Jerusalem, killing the prophets and stoning those who are sent to you! How often would I have gathered your children together as a hen gathers her brood under her wings, and you would not!"
Matthew 23:13	"But woe to you, scribes and Pharisees, hypocrites! because you shut

the kingdom of heaven against men; for you neither enter yourselves, nor allow those who would enter to go in."

Matthew 23:33-34

"You serpents, you brood of vipers, how are you to escape being sentenced to hell? Therefore I send you prophets and wise men and scribes, some of whom you will kill and crucify, and some you will scourge in your synagogues and persecute from town to town . . ."

Matthew 23:27-31

"Woe to you, scribes and Pharisees, hypocrites! for you are like whitewashed tombs, which outwardly appear beautiful, but within they are full of dead men's bones and all uncleanness. So you also outwardly appear righteous to men, but within you are full of hypocrisy and iniquity.

"Woe to you, scribes and Pharisees, hypocrites! for you blind the tombs of the prophets and adorn the monuments of the righteous, saying, 'If we had lived in the days of our fathers, we would not have taken part with them in shedding the blood of the prophets.' Thus you witness against yourselves, that you are sons of those who murdered the prophets."

Mark 7:6-8 "Well did Isaiah prophesy of you hypocrites, as it is written,
> 'This people honors me with their lips,
> but their heart is far from me;
> in vain do they worship me,
> teaching as doctrines the precepts of men.'

You leave the commandment of God, and hold fast the tradition of men."

Bahá'í References

Consider the past. How many, both high and low, have, at all times, yearningly awaited the advent of the Manifestations of God in the sanctified persons of His chosen Ones. How often have they expected His coming, how frequently have they prayed that the breeze of divine mercy might blow, and the promised Beauty step forth from behind the veil of concealment, and be made manifest to all the world. And whensoever the portals of grace did open, and the clouds of divine bounty did rain upon mankind, and the light of the Unseen did shine above the horizon of celestial might, they all denied Him,

and turned away from His face—the face of God Himself. Refer ye, to verify this truth, to that which hath been recorded in every sacred Book.
Bahá'u'lláh
Kitáb-i-Iqán, p. 4

Leaders of religion, in every age, have hindered their people from attaining the shores of eternal salvation, inasmuch as they held the reins of authority in their mighty grasp. Some for the lust of leadership, others through want of knowledge and understanding, have been the cause of the deprivation of the people. By their sanction and authority, every Prophet of God hath drunk from the chalice of sacrifice, and winged His flight unto the heights of glory. What unspeakable cruelties they that have occupied the seats of authority and learning have inflicted upon the true Monarchs of the world, those Gems of divine virtue! Content with a transitory dominion, they have deprived themselves of an everlasting sovereignty.
Bahá'u'lláh
Kitáb-i-Iqán, p. 15

For what reason do they refuse to embrace the Truth, and allow certain traditions, the significance of which they have failed to grasp, to withhold them from the recognition of the Revelation of God and His Beauty, and to cause them to dwell in the infernal abyss? Such things are to be attributed to naught but the faithlessness of the divines and doctors of the age.

Bahá'u'lláh
Kitáb-i-Iqán, pp. 247-48

These leaders, owing to their immersion in selfish desires, and their pursuit of transitory and sordid things, have regarded these divine Luminaries as being opposed to the standards of their knowledge and understanding, and the opponents of their ways and judgments. As they have literally interpreted the Word of God, and the sayings and traditions of the Letters of Unity, and expounded them according to their own deficient understanding, they have therefore deprived themselves and all their people of the bountiful showers of the grace and mercies of God.

Bahá'u'lláh
Kitáb-i-Iqán, p. 82

Not one Prophet of God was made manifest Who did not fall victim to the relentless hate, to the denunciation, denial, and execration of the clerics of His day!

Bahá'u'lláh
Kitáb-i-Iqán, p. 165

How many men and women awaited the manifestation of the Messiah after Moses? Yet when His beauty shone forth and His face appeared, they (the people) did not recognize Him, but continued to

follow the superstitions of the Pharisees, who used to say: "Where is the throne of David, the Glorious? Where is his iron rod? Where are his innumerable hosts? Where are his attacking armies? Where are the angels of heaven?"
'Abdu'l-Bahá
Tablets of 'Abdu'l-Bahá, p. 230

Consider those who opposed the Son [Jesus], when He came unto them with sovereignty and power. How many the Pharisees who were waiting to behold Him, and were lamenting over their separation from Him! And yet, when the fragrance of His coming was wafted over them, and His beauty was unveiled, they turned aside from Him and disputed with Him.
Bahá'u'lláh, quoted in
The Promised Day is Come, p. 31

They are even as the Pharisees who both prayed and fasted, and then did sentence Jesus Christ to death.
'Abdu'l-Bahá
Selections from the Writings of 'Abdu'l-Bahá, p. 174

Blessed are the just souls who seek the truth. But failing justice, the people attack, dispute and openly deny the evidence, like the Pharisees who, at the manifestation of Christ, denied with the greatest obstinacy the explanations of Christ and of His disciples. They obscured Christ's Cause before the ignorant people, saying, "These prophecies are not of Jesus, but of the Promised One Who shall come later, according to the conditions mentioned in the Bible." Some of these conditions were that He must have a kingdom, be seated on the throne of David, enforce the Law of the Bible, and manifest such justice that the wolf and lamb shall gather at the same spring.

And thus they prevented the people from knowing Christ."

'Abdu'l-Bahá
Some Answered Questions, pp. 71-2

How great, how very great is the Cause! How very fierce the onslaught of all the peoples and kindreds of the earth. Ere long shall the clamor of the multitude throughout Africa, throughout America, the cry of the European and of the Turk, the groaning of India and China, be heard from far and near. One and all, they shall arise with all their power to resist His Cause. Then shall the knights of the Lord, assisted by His grace from on high, strengthened by faith, aided by the power of understanding, and reinforced by the legions of the Covenant, arise and make manifest the truth of the verse: "Behold the confusion that hath befallen the tribes of the defeated!"

'Abdu'l-Bahá, quoted in
The World Order of Bahá'u'lláh, p. 17

THE SOWER
(Matthew 13:3-23)

THE SELECT FEW

Despite opposition to the Manifestations of God, there are always a select few who, by the bounty of God, are aided to acquire the Spirit of Faith. These few believers always manage to withstand the trials, difficulties, and ordeals that assail them. Those who attain to this station remain firm and steadfast in the path of God. Their rewards, as all the scriptures confirm, are beyond description—spiritual rebirth, love, rapture, and ecstasy enkindled in the believer's heart.

Biblical References

Matthew 22:14   "For many are called, but few are chosen."

Matthew 7:21   "Not every one who says to me, 'Lord, Lord,' shall enter the kingdom of heaven, but he who does the will of my Father who is in heaven."

Luke 6:22	"Blessed are you when men hate you, and when they exclude you and revile you, and cast out your name as evil, on account of the Son of man! Rejoice in that day, and leap for joy, for behold, your reward is great in heaven; for so their fathers did to the prophets."

Bahá'í References

By the sorrows which afflict the beauty of the All-Glorious! Such is the station ordained for the true believer that if to an extent smaller than a needle's eye the glory of that station were to be unveiled to mankind, every beholder would be consumed away in his longing to attain it. For this reason it hath been decreed that in this earthly life the full measure of the glory of his own station should remain concealed from the eyes of such a believer.

Bahá'u'lláh, quoted in
World Order of Bahá'u'lláh, p. 108

This is a Day great and blessed. Whatsoever was hidden in man is today being revealed. The station of man is great, were he to cling to truth and righteousness and be firm and steadfast in the Cause. Before the God of Mercy, a true man appears like unto heaven. The sun and moon of that heaven are his sight and hearing and its stars are his shining attributes. His station is the highest and his signs are the educator of the world.

Bahá'u'lláh, quoted in
Bahá'í World Faith, p. 208

Know thou, of a truth, that if the soul of man hath walked in the ways of God, it will, assuredly, return and be gathered to the glory of the Beloved. By the righteousness of God! It shall attain a station such as no pen can depict, or tongue describe. The soul that hath remained faithful to the Cause of God, and stood unwaveringly firm in His Path shall, after his ascension, be possessed of such power that all the worlds which the Almighty hath created can benefit through him. Such a soul provideth, at the bidding of the Ideal King and Divine Educator, the pure leaven that leaventh the world of being, and furnisheth the power through which the arts and wonders of the world are made manifest. Those souls that are the symbols of detachment are the leaven of the world.

Bahá'u'lláh
Gleanings, p. 161

TWO PROPHETS TO APPEAR

The Holy Books make reference to two Manifestations of God who are either to appear contemporaneously, or one shortly after the other. Often the prophecies indicate that one of these will prepare the way for the other.

In the Old Testament, there are references made to the Messiah and the Lord of Hosts. In the Gospels, there are the promises of the return of Christ and the return of Elijah. (Matthew 17:10-11) In the Qur'an also, reference is made to two who are to appear, the Mihdí and the Messiah.

Biblical References

Malachi 3:1	"Behold, I send my messenger to prepare the way before me, and the Lord whom you seek will suddenly come to his temple; the messenger of the covenant in whom you delight, behold, he is coming, says the LORD of hosts."

Malachi 4:5	"Behold, I will send you Elijah the prophet before the great and terrible day of the LORD comes."
Zechariah 4:11-14	Then I said to him, "What are these two olive trees on the right and the left of the lampstand?" And a second time I said to him, "What are these two branches of the olive trees, which are beside the two golden pipes from which the oil is poured out?" He said to me, "Do you not know what these are?" I said, "No, my lord." Then he said, "These are the two anointed who stand by the Lord of the whole earth."
Revelation 9:12	The first woe has passed; behold, two woes are still to come.
Revelation 11:3-4	And I will grant my two witnesses power to prophesy . . . These are the two olive trees and the two lampstands which stand before the Lord of the earth.
Revelation 11:14	The second woe has passed; behold, the third woe is soon to come.

TWO PROPHETS

Bahá'í References

St. John the Divine had himself, with reference to these two successive Revelations, clearly prophesied: "The second woe is past; and behold the third woe cometh quickly." *"This third woe,"* 'Abdu'l-Bahá, commenting upon this verse, has explained, *"is the day of the Manifestation of Bahá'u'lláh, the Day of God, and it is near to the day of the appearance of the Báb."*

Shoghi Effendi,
God Passes By, p. 92

All the peoples of the world are awaiting two Manifestations, Who must be contemporaneous; all wait for the fulfillment of this promise. In the Bible the Jews have the promise of the Lord of Hosts and the Messiah; in the Gospel the return of Christ and Elijah is promised.

In the religion of Muhammad there is the promise of the Mihdí and the Messiah, and it is the same with the Zoroastrian and the other religions, but if we relate these matters in detail, it would take too long. The essential fact is that all are promised two Manifestations, Who will come, one following on the other.

'Abdu'l-Bahá,
Some Answered Questions, p. 39

Lo! The Father is come, and that which ye were promised in the Kingdom is fulfilled! This is the

Word which the Son concealed, when to those around Him he said: "Ye cannot bear it now." And when the appointed time was fulfilled and the Hour had struck, the Word shone forth above the horizon of the Will of God. Beware, O followers of the Son, that ye cast it not behind your backs. Take ye fast hold of it. Better is this for you than all that ye possess. Verily He is nigh unto them that do good. The Hour which We had concealed from the knowledge of the peoples of the earth and of the favoured angels hath come to pass. Say, verily, He hath testified of Me, and I do testify of Him. Indeed, He hath purposed no one other than Me. Unto this beareth witness every fair-minded and understanding soul.

Bahá'u'lláh.
Tablets of Bahá'u'lláh, p. 11

THE MAN WHOSE NAME IS THE BRANCH

Another of the amazing bounties which have been conferred upon us in this Day by the mercy of God is the prophecy concerning "the man whose name is the Branch." This man will build the temple of the Lord and will rule wisely, with justice and righteousness, according to the prophecies.

For Bahá'ís, this man was 'Abdu'l-Bahá, the son of Bahá'u'lláh, designated by his Father as the Most Great Branch.

Biblical References

Zechariah 3:8	Hear now, O Joshua the high priest, you and your friends who sit before you, for they are men of good omen: behold, I will bring my servant the Branch.
Zechariah 6:12-13	Thus says the Lord of hosts, "Behold, the man whose name is the Branch: for he shall grow up

in his place, and he shall build the temple of the Lord. It is he who shall build the temple of the Lord, and shall bear royal honor, and shall sit and rule upon his throne."

Jeremiah 23:5   "Behold, the days are coming, says the Lord, when I will raise up for David a righteous Branch, and he shall reign as king and deal wisely, and shall execute justice and righteousness in the land."

Bahá'í References

When the ocean of My presence hath ebbed and the Book of My Revelation is ended, turn your faces towards Him Whom God hath purposed, Who hath branched from this Ancient Root.

Bahá'u'lláh, quoted in
World Order of Bahá'u'lláh, p. 134

There hath branched from the Sadratu'l-Muntahá this sacred and glorious Being, this Branch of Holiness; well is it with him that hath sought His shelter and abideth beneath His shadow. Verily the Limb of the Law of God hath sprung forth from this Root which God hath firmly implanted in the Ground of His Will, and Whose Branch hath been so uplifted as to encompass the whole of creation. Magnified be He, therefore, for this sublime, this blessed, this mighty, this exalted Handiwork!

Bahá'u'lláh, quoted in
World Order of Bahá'u'lláh, p. 135

You have written that there is a difference among the believers concerning the "Second Coming of Christ." Gracious God! Time and again this question hath arisen, and its answer hath emanated in a clear and irrefutable statement from the pen of 'Abdu'l-Bahá, that what is meant in the prophecies by the "Lord of Hosts" . . . is the Blessed Perfection (Bahá'u'lláh) and His holiness the Exalted One (the Báb). My name is 'Abdu'l-Bahá [Servant of Bahá]. My qualification is 'Abdu'l-Bahá. My reality is 'Abdu'l-Bahá. My praise is 'Abdu'l-Bahá. Thraldom to the Blessed Perfection is my glorious and refulgent diadem, and servitude to all the human race is my perpetual religion . . . No name, no title, no mention, no commendation have I, nor will ever have, except 'Abdu'l-Bahá. This is my longing. This is my greatest yearning. This is my eternal life. This is my everlasting glory.

'Abdu'l-Bahá, quoted in
World Order of Bahá'u'lláh, p. 139

FUTURE MANIFESTATIONS OF GOD

Just as all the previous Prophets and Manifestations of God have foretold the coming of the One who would appear after them, so Bahá'u'lláh has spoken of Prophets to come. However, He has made it clear that no true prophet will come before the expiration of a thousand years after His Revelation.

Bahá'í References

"God hath sent down His Messengers to succeed to Moses and Jesus, and he will continue to do so till the 'end that hath no end'; so that His grace may, from the heaven of Divine bounty, be continually vouchsafed to mankind."

"I am not apprehensive for My own self, My fears are for Him Who will be sent down unto you after Me—Him Who will be invested with great sovereignty and mighty dominion." . . .

"By those words which I have revealed, Myself is not intended, but rather He Who will come after

Me. To it is witness God, the All-Knowing." "Deal not with Him, as ye have dealt with Me."
Bahá'u'lláh, quoted in
World Order of Bahá'u'lláh, pp. 116-17

Whoso layeth claim to a Revelation direct from God, ere the expiration of a full thousand years, such a man is assuredly a lying imposter. We pray God that He may graciously assist him to retract and repudiate such claim. Should he repent, God will, no doubt, forgive him. If, however, he persisteth in his error, God will, assuredly, send down one who will deal mercilessly with him. Terrible, indeed, is God in punishing! Whosover interpreteth this verse otherwise than its obvious meaning is deprived of the spirit of God and His mercy which encompasseth all created things. Fear God, and follow not your idle fancies. Nay, rather follow the bidding of your Lord, the Almightly, the All-Wise.
Bahá'u'lláh,
Gleanings, p. 346

Be ye assured, moreover, that the works and acts of each and every one of these Manifestations of God, nay whatever pertaineth unto them, and whatsoever they may manifest in the future, are all ordained by God, and are a reflection of His Will and Purpose.
Bahá'u'lláh,
Gleanings, p. 59

"Concerning the Manifestations that will come down in the future 'in the shadow of the clouds,' know verily that in so far as their relation to the source of their inspiration is concerned they are under the shadow of the Ancient Beauty. In their relation, however, to the age in which they appear, each and every one of them 'doeth whatsoever He willeth.'"

'Abdu'l-Bahá, quoted in
World Order of Bahá'u'lláh, p. 111

SELECTED BIBLIOGRAPHY

Selections from the Bible are taken from the Revised Standard Version of the Old and New Testaments.

From the Writings of Bahá'u'lláh:

Epistle to the Son of the Wolf. Trans. by Shoghi Effendi. Wilmette, Ill.: Bahá'í Publishing Trust, 1962.

Gleanings from the Writings of Bahá'u'lláh. Comp. and trans. by Shoghi Effendi. 2nd Rev. Ed. Wilmette, Ill.: Bahá'í Publishing Trust, 1976.

The Kitáb-i-Iqán, The Book of Certitude. Trans. by Shoghi Effendi. 2nd Ed. Wilmette, Ill.: Bahá'í Publishing Trust, 1954.

A Synopsis and Codification of the Kitáb-i-Aqdás. Haifa: Bahá'í World Centre, 1973.

From the Writings of the Báb:

Selections from the Writings of the Báb. Trans. by Habib Taherzadeh. Haifa: Bahá'í World Centre, 1976.

From the Writings of 'Abdu'l-Bahá:

The Promulgation of Universal Peace. 2nd Ed. Wilmette, Ill.: Bahá'í Publishing Trust, 1982.
Secret of Divine Civilization. 1970 Ed. Wilmette, Ill.:Bahá'í Publishing Trust, 1970.
Selections from the Writings of 'Abdu'l-Bahá. Haifa: Bahá'í World Centre, 1978.
Some Answered Questions. 1964 Ed. Wilmette, Ill.: Bahá'í Publishing Trust, 1964.
Tablets of Abdul-Baha Abbas. Chicago: Bahai Publishing Society, 1909-1916.

Compilations:

Bahá'í World Faith. 2nd Ed. Wilmette, Ill.: Bahá'í Publishing Trust, 1956.
The Divine Art of Living. Comp. by Mabel Hyde Paine. Rev. Ed. Wilmette, Ill.: Bahá'í Publishing Trust, 1956.

The Writings of Shoghi Effendi:

The Dawn-Breakers: Nabíl's Narrative of the Early Days of the Bahá'í Faith. Trans. by Shoghi Effendi. Wilmette, Ill.: Bahá'í Publishing Trust, 1932.
God Passes By. Wilmette, Ill.: Bahá'í Publishing Committee, 1944.
The Promised Day Is Come. 1961 Ed. Wilmette, Ill.: Bahá'í Publishing Trust, 1961.

Other works:

William Sears. *Thief in the Night*. London: George Ronald, 1961.

Illustrations for this book are reprinted from *The Doré Bible Illustrations: 241 Illustrations by Gustave Doré* (New York: Dover Publications, Inc., 1974) and from *The New Testament: A Pictorial Archive from Nineteenth Century Sources: 311 Copyright-Free Illustrations* (New York: Dover Publications Inc., 1986).

Acknowledgements (continued from page iv)

compilations, *Bahá'í World Faith*, Copyright 1943, © 1956, 1976; *The Divine Art of Living*, Copyright 1944, © 1972, 1974. By Shoghi Effendi, *The Dawnbreakers: Nabíl's Narrative of the Early Days of the Bahá'í Faith*, Copyright 1932, © 1970; *God Passes By*, Copyright 1944, © 1957; *The Promised Day is Come*, Copyright 1941, ©1969, 1980; *The World Order of Bahá'u'lláh*, Copyright 1938, © 1955, 1974. Other works, J.E. Esslemont, *Bahá'u'lláh and the New Era*, Copyright 1950, © 1970, 1980.